APPLIED CHRISTIANITY

A HANDBOOK OF 500 GOOD WORKS

Katheryn Maddox Haddad

Other Books by this Author

CHRISTIAN LIFE
Applied Christianity: Handbook 500 Good Works
You Can Be a Hero Alone
Worship Changes Since 1st Century + Worship 1sr Century Way
The Best of Alexander Campbell's Millennial Harbinger
Inside the Hearts of Bible Women-Reader+Audio+Leader
The Lord's Supper: 52 Readings with Prayers

BIBLE TEXTS
Revelation: A Love Letter From God
The Holy Spirit: 592 Verses Examined
Was Jesus God? (Why Evil)
365 Life-Changing Scriptures Day by Date
Love Letters of Jesus & His Bride, Ecclesia (Song of Solomon)
Christianity or Islam? The Contrast
The Road to Heaven

FUN BOOKS
Bible Puzzles, Bible Song Book, Bible Numbers

TOUCHING GOD SERIES
365 Golden Bible Thoughts: God's Heart to Yours
365 Pearls of Wisdom: God's Soul to Yours
365 Silver-Winged Prayers: Your Spirit to God's

SURVEY SERIES: EASY BIBLE WORKBOOKS
→Old Testament & New Testament Surveys
→Questions You Have Asked-Part I & II

HISTORICAL RESEARCH BIBLE
for Novel, Screenwriter, Documentary & Thesis Writers

HISTORICAL NOVELS & STORYBOOKS
Series of 8: They Met Jesus
Ongoing Series of 8: Intrepid Men of God
Mysteries of the Empire with Klaudius & Hektor
Christmas: They Rocked the Cradle that Rocked the World
Series of 8: A Child's Life of Christ
Series of 10: A Child's Bible Heroes
Series of 8: A Child's Bible Kids
Series of 10: A Child's Bible Ladies

GENEALOGY: Climb Your Family Tree w/o Falling Out
Volume I & 2: Beginner-Intermediate & Colonial-Medieval

Cover Design by Sharon Lavy, Deposit Photos
Copyright ℮ 2014 Katheryn Maddox Haddad
ISBN- 978-1-948462-86-0
NORTHERN LIGHTS PUBLISHING HOUSE

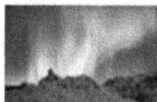

Printed in the United States
Printings 1976, 2011, 2014

In Praise of
APPLIED CHRISTIANITY:
A Handbook of 500 Good Works

* * * * * EVA P. SCOTT.

Need an **Idea** for Something to Do to **Encourage Others**? This book gives you ideas to implement for doing good works. It is not so much telling you why you should do them but gives suggestions of things to do to **help others**.

* * * * AMAZON CUSTOMER.

This was a very good book about all the different way of **influencing people** for the Gospel. So many simple things even people who can't leave the house can do. I found it **very helpful.**

Table of Contents

A Brief Explanation

This is a "Handbook" of good works. It is designed as a manual to be referred to as life circumstances change.

Not every part will apply to the opportunities of every person. It was written with those in mind who worship in small congregations all the way up to large thriving congregations. It was written for those who live in small towns and for people in large cities. It was written for new Christians as well as mature Christians; for young people as well as older people. It is for those who are strong and active physically, as well as those who are completely paralyzed and bedridden.

In every instance, step-by-step suggestions are made to carry out a particular good work. But, of course, these are only suggestions and may be altered according to the individual. These are merely examples to show ways which have worked for various people.

Finally, to paraphrase what Paul the Apostle once said in I Corinthians 9:23 in the Bible, this book will help Christians be *"made all things to all men, that [you] might by all means save some."*

1 ~ LOOK AROUND, ACT, & REACT

Have you ever wondered why so many churches are relatively inactive out in the world? Perhaps we have overlooked something: Inactivity is what we in our classrooms were taught years ago and what we in turn teach when we become the teachers ourselves in the next generation. How?

We teach by our actions that Christianity is (1) going to worship services, (2) listening, (3) discussing, (4) going home. For all the world knows, they see us entering a building and coming out again; and that's the end of that! We are not any different and they are not any different. No wonder people of the world think Christianity is boring. If that is all we do, then it is. But it doesn't have to be.

Studying alone is not Christianity ~ never was and never will be. Faith alone is not Christianity either. They are both dead by themselves (James 2:17). Christian worship services are spiritual feasts where we eat of the bread of life. But if all we do is eat with no exercise, we get spiritually fat and lazy. Now who wants that? No one, really, of course.

The purpose of the worship assemblies is specifically spelled out in Hebrews 10. It is ironic how we use the first half of verse 25 by itself to reprimand those who do not attend all our worship gatherings when they could if they wanted to. By putting this with the rest of verse 25 we condemn many so-called "active" Christians also who are missing the whole purpose of the assemblies. Notice:

[WHO?] *Let us draw near to God with a sincere heart in full assurance of faith, having our hearts sprinkled to cleanse us from a guilty conscience and having our bodies washed with pure water.* [WHAT?] *Let us hold unswervingly to the hope we profess, for he who promised is faithful. And let us consider how we may spur one another on toward love and good deeds.* [WHEN/HOW?] *Let us not give up meeting together, as some are in the habit of doing, but let us encourage one another ~ and all the more as you see the Day approaching.* [WHY?] *If we deliberately keep on sinning after we have received the knowledge of the truth, no sacrifice for sins is left, but only a fearful expectation of judgment and of raging fire that will consume the enemies of God.*

Let us show each other how to love and be filled with good

works, and then encourage each other to do them. Otherwise we sin willfully; there no longer remains a sacrifice for our sins but rather a terrifying judgment. Remember, the devils know all about God and believe and tremble (James 2:19), and it does not benefit them anything. Let us put behind us always being a learner by just "being there every time the doors are open;" for that only makes us *a hearer of the word and not a doer...like unto a man beholding his natural face in a glass; for he beholds himself, and goes his way, and straightway forgets what manner of man he was* (James 1:23,24).

Do not misunderstand. Being at the worship services and Bible classes is extremely important and should not be minimized for one moment. In fact, Hebrews 10 states that we should assemble ourselves together "all the more" as we see the day of judgment approaching. Actually, the early Christians met daily (Acts 2:46). But as the old popular song asks, "Is that all there is?" No, of course not.

As important as these times of study and worship are, as important as eating is, this is only the beginning, not the end in itself. This provides the spiritual bread of life so we can go out with spiritual energy and be able to do our Christian daily works. In fact, it creates a cycle. The more Christian works we do, the more spiritual food we need, the more we want to attend Christian assemblies so we can get more spiritual food to go out and do more work.

Actually, once you become vitally involved with daily Christian works, the worship hours will develop a new meaning to you. Suddenly you will realize that it does not matter that much if the song leader drags the songs, the Bible reader stumbles over a word or two, the preacher preaches the same sermon again. For while you are doing all your Christian works during the week, you are loving in action, you are showing people God (who is Love), you are Love's ambassador. Thus you learn to love your Christian brothers and sisters so much that you do not even realize they are not perfect. 1 Corinthians 13:5 states that love is not provoked by the weaknesses of others, or by anything else. Love does not notice, but prevails.

Out in the world day by day you will be loving others so much that you will be overwhelmed by the tremendous capacity of love you feel from God through those around you. And you will want to adore and sing praises to him and thank him, and learn more and more about him all the time ~ *all the more as you see the day approaching.* It will no longer be a matter of HAVING to go to worship, but LOOKING FORWARD to going because your very heart would burst if you could not.

In the Old Testament, sacrifice was the center of worship. In the New Testament era sacrifice is still the center of worship. Hebrews 13:15,16 states, *Through Jesus, therefore, let us continually offer to God a sacrifice of praise - the fruit of lips that confess his name. And do not forget to do good and to share with others, for with such sacrifices God is pleased.* Not only do we sacrifice the fruit of our lips in worship, but also the incense of prayer (Revelation 8:4) and the incense of giving (Philippians 4:15,18).

Perhaps you do not need any encouragement to do or keep up your good works; but maybe those others who do need it will be there at the assembly waiting for you to come and encourage them. On the other hand, there will be times when you will be needing encouragement; this happens to everyone. According to Hebrews 10:25, we encourage one another when we assemble together. We must never let the other person down. That is God's plan, God's way.

The worship period is only the beginning of our worship, the beginning of our service. In the worship assembly, we offer the sacrifice of our lips, our ears and our minds. Notice carefully Romans 12:1. *Therefore, I urge you, brothers, in view of God's mercy, to offer your bodies as living sacrifices, holy and pleasing to God ~ which is your spiritual worship.* The King James Version states that it is *your reasonable service.* It is only reasonable to expect a Christian to be full of good works and to encourage others to be. That is the fulfillment of worship to God.

Matthew 7:16,20 both quote Jesus as saying, *By their fruits you will recognize them.* John 15:16 recalls Jesus explaining to his disciples, *I chose you to go and bear fruit ~ fruit that will last.* Romans 7:4 tells us what our purpose in life is once we are born anew as Christians. *So, my brothers, you also died to the law through the body of Christ, that you might belong to another, to him who was raised from the dead, in order that we might bear fruit to God.*

Are you bearing fruit? Are you a Christian in every way? Do you claim to be Christ-like? Jesus said in John 15:5, *I am the vine; you are the branches. If a man remains in me and I in him, he will bear much fruit; apart from me you can do nothing.* Are you apart from Jesus? Have you been doing nothing? Jesus went on to warn in verse 6, *If anyone does not abide in me, he is thrown away as a branch, and dries up; and they gather them, and cast them into the fire, and they are burned.* Jesus said we must bring forth fruit. He commanded it.

Let us not be one of those to whom he said, And why do you call me 'Lord, Lord,' and do not what I say? Matthew 7:21 gives this warning: *Not everyone who says to me, "Lord!" "Lord!" will enter the kingdom of heaven, but only he who does the will of my Father who is in heaven.*

We often use the above verses to illustrate that, if some religious groups do not organize themselves according to the instructions in the Bible, do not become Christians according to the Bible, and do not hold worship services according to the examples of the Bible, they should question their salvation.

This may be true. But we must not forget that it applies just as strongly to those who call out, "Lord!" yet do not go into the world around them and bring forth some fruit. 1 John 3:18 gives this gentle warning, *Dear children, let us not love with words or tongue but with actions and in truth*

Today, dare to put your Christianity into practice. Today, and tomorrow, and tomorrow, and every day until it has spanned the rest of your life. Make the decision for today, and for tomorrow's today, one day at a time. You will soon find that such practice becomes a driving force in your life which you cannot stop. You will become addicted to it! 1 Corinthians 16:15 speaks of a family who had *Addicted themselves to the ministry of the saints* (KJV). Yes, this can happen to you, and It isn't that hard to do.

How can you get started if you have not been used to doing daily good works and bringing forth these fruits? Again, go back to Hebrews 10:22-27. Assemble yourself more and more with other Christians so you may give and receive encouragement. This is the first vital step. Your Bible classes and worship services are two forms of assembling.

Other forms of assembling include setting aside one or two days a week to get with someone you can work with and spend time visiting people. Have class projects, and take some of the work home with you to do before the next class time. Have a quiet time set aside each day at home for private works if not employed outside your home.

Try to do as much as possible by twos or more. We need each other. This will help you not put things off you know you should be doing and deep down really do want to do. *Anyone, then, who knows the good he ought to do and doesn't do it, sins* James 4:17). Jesus recommended it. The disciples practiced it. This is God's wisdom. Do not depend on yourself alone. The early Christians were always together doing some sort of good work. *Every day they continued to meet together in the temple courts. They broke bread in their homes and ate together with glad and sincere hearts, praising God and enjoying the favor of all the people. And the Lord added to their number daily those who were being saved* (Acts 2:46,47).

You can't miss it! If you are daily teaching and doing good works with each other, there will be many conversions to Christ, for people will notice the church (kingdom of Christians) think favorably of it, and want to be a part of it so they may have the happiness and peace you have. That's how it works. It did in the first century; it does now.

Even the contribution at your congregation will go up automatically, spontaneously. Not because someone told you and the other Christians to, but because you will be so involved in good works, you will see more and more needs even in a monetary form. You will want to give so you through your money, as well as time, will be able to accomplish those good works.

We too often think of giving as something we have to do or the preacher will harass us. (Sometimes, though, if a preacher preaches on it twice a year, we think of it as harassing. Guilty consciences?) After you get to work, you no longer think of giving as putting some money in a cold impersonal plate, and it going to pay for just the building, the utilities, salaries, and class books. Your money will be doing many good works and you will be glad.

Giving of our money is just one part of the giving and seed planting involved in your Christian life.

Remember, you are to offer your body as a living sacrifice. Everything you give is just a part of that sacrifice. And the more of one thing a person gives - such as time - the more of other things that person wants to give. Our whole way of thinking changes.

Every time you buy something, you will catch yourself thinking, "How can I use this for God?" After all, everything we have is God's anyway (James 1:17). You will find you can use your new house to entertain in. You can use your new stove to new refrigerator for cold drinks, storing fruits, vegetables, etc. to share with those you enjoy being with and enjoy helping. You can use your new car to pick up people to go to Bible class, to take to the doctor, to take shopping, etc. When you get new clothes, you can give your outgrown ones to someone who needs them. When your children buy new toys, they can share them with their friends. And, of course, everything we have been blessed with through the years -not necessarily recently ~ we can share with others. After all, God is sharing them with us!

In another sense, Jesus said in Matthew 25:34-40: *Then the King will say to those on his right, "Come, you who are blessed by my Father; take your inheritance, the kingdom prepared for you since the creation of the world. For I was hungry and you gave me something to eat, I was thirsty and you gave me something to drink, I was a stranger and you invited me in, I needed clothes and you clothed me, I was sick and you looked after me, I was in prison and you came to visit me." Then the righteous will answer him, "Lord, when did we see you hungry and feed you, or thirsty and give you something to drink? When did we see you a stranger and invite you in, or needing clothes and clothe you? When did we see you sick or in prison and go to visit you?" The King will reply, "I tell you the truth, whatever you did for one of these brethren of mine, you did for me."*

In the midst of beginning your new life of service, you must be aware of subtle and not-so-subtle forces to stop you. There will always be those weak Christians who may criticize you for all your good works. Or shall we call it persecution? They may claim all kinds of things about your motives for doing the good works. They might even make up a few things about you that are false. As hard as it is to say - it is harder even to do - you must never let this discourage you and stop you. Instead, turn it around and use it as a spiritual thermometer to see how well you are doing as a Christian. Remember, the more good David did to Saul, the more Saul hated him and tried to kill him. And the more good Jesus did, the more the "faith-only" religious people hated him and tried to kill him.

Blessed are those who are persecuted because of righteousness, for theirs is the kingdom of heaven. Blessed are when people insult you, persecute you and falsely say all kinds of evil against you because of me. Rejoice and be glad, because great is your reward in heaven, for in the same way they persecuted the prophets who were before you. You are the salt of the earth (Matthew 5:10-13a). See there? It's your thermometer. Worldly Christians or weak Christians (same thing) certainly criticize you. The more you work, the more Satan will try to get you to stop - even through your own friends and family.

Perhaps it is that those who shout the loudest are those who deep down envy you the most. so take note of those people. Get better acquainted with them, and invite them to do some of these Christian works with you. After a while, they will probably say that you have changed and aren't so overbearing and all those other things they perhaps used to call you. Actually, what it really will be is that they will have changed and will see you now through the eyes of love and brotherliness, a fellow worker. This has happened over and over through the history of the world, and is probably the best way to get rid of a critic ~ make them a participant.

Lastly, be careful of your motives. At first your motives to do good works will be good, but as more and more people begin to condemn or praise you for doing them (they will do both), your motives may change you into being a people pleaser rather than a God pleaser. Always keep in mind 1 Corinthians 13:3: If I give all I possess to the poor and surrender my body to the flames, but have not love, I gain nothing.

Whenever you go out to do a good work, refer to yourself as so-and-so from the church or the body of Christ. Your motives will not be as easily misunderstood, and you will always be reminding even yourself of your purpose in doing these things. Christ is your purpose. You are a fellow worker with him (2 Corinthians 6:1). By glorifying his church, you will be glorifying Christ, the Head. And this is what you want above all else on earth.

Now take the challenge! Of course you can do it! God bless you!

2 ~ LETTER WRITING

If you only have ten minutes on your lunch hour at work, you are too young or too old to drive a car or just don't have access to one; if you are confined to your home due to illness or children; or if for any other reason you may not be able to leave your work or home to do your Christian works, you can still write

Whole nations have been influenced by what is written. The whole world has been influenced by what was written by the hand of God in his holy writings, the Bible. Not one word ever written by one and read by another has ever missed Influencing the thinking of the reader. The reader may agree or disagree or be unimpressed, but it still influences their thinking. You can and will influence others for Christ by what you write.

Begin, first, by writing to a Christian supply store at a Christian college if you do not know of any nearby. If you do not know the address of the college, most post offices know where public institutions are anyway and will see that your letter is delivered. Ask them to mail you a supply of get-well cards, sympathy cards, thinking-of-you cards, birthday cards, wedding cards, and baby cards. Try to get cards that have a scripture quotation in them. You can still get a box of 20 cards for about 25c per card. So buying by the box is always more economical. Get-well, birthday, and thinking-of-you cards you will probably use the most. A box of assorted cards will give you a few each of the others.

Now, while you're waiting for your cards, read your newspaper. There are articles in it about mostly bad things - crimes and death. Instead of dreading to read your newspaper because it depresses you, turn it around and view it as a plea for help from a multitude of people.

Were there any people involved in robberies, or drugs, or murders? Makes you shudder to think of it close to home, doesn't it? How do you think the families of these people feel when it hits their homes? You've got a telephone book and a telephone. Use them to get their home address if you need to. Then write the family a note. Tell them how sorry you are. Tell them that you are praying for them. (Be sure it is the truth before you say it though.) Copy some scriptures of encouragement for them (most people don't look up scriptures on their own). Find some way to mention the church in your letter. Say something like, "Our minister or elders will be happy to come to your home and pray with you; they are _____. Or I could come." Or you may just sign your name, and under it write the congregation of which you are a member.

You may also want to write a note to those who are in jail because of what they are accused of, perhaps awaiting trial. They may not act interested in your note, and just say you are some kind of weird religious fanatic. But so what? That's just what they may say. What they really think deep down is often something much different -fear, questionings, resentment, confusion, irrelevance of religion, feelings of hate and lack of love.

If you copy a few scriptures on the love and encouragement they need, always remember God said his word would not return to him void. Isaiah 55:11 tells us this. *So shall my word be that goes forth out of my mouth: It shall not return unto me void, but it shall accomplish that which I please, and it shall prosper in the thing whereto I sent it.*

Do not expect a reply to most of these letters you write. Just remember, God's word will not return to him void, and your sending them his word will not return to God void either. If they do reply, write them again and ask them if there is anything they need. Again, they are likely not to tell you even if there is, but they will probably indeed be in need, especially families whose breadwinner is in trouble. Contact one of your elders or minister or benevolent committee, show them their reply, and perhaps they will want to visit these people to see if they need anything. (More on this in the chapter on benevolence.) This is the time they will most need true friends, and probably find themselves without them, for such families often find themselves bitter during such a time.

Read on in the newspaper. There is the obituary column. When your cards arrive, send a sympathy card to the family and write a little message on it or enclose a letter. Have you been through similar deaths in your family? Tell them so. Tell them you understand. Copy word for word some scriptures to help comfort them.

You may think they would not be interested in a card from a stranger. Sometimes a card from a stranger who cares, even though they do not know you personally, is one of the most touching things a person can receive. "They don't even know me," they will tell someone. "But they wrote anyway. They actually care, and don't know me from Adam! I wonder what makes them like that?" You have introduced the real Christ to them. You care because Jesus cares. They will want what you have, and when you begin showing them the scriptures on Christianity (if your correspondence continues) they will want those too. Jesus did it the same way. He demonstrated his love, and then he explained it and showed them how they could be the same way.

Next you come to the wedding page. What a surprise to receive a wedding greeting from someone they don't even know. You may be able to enclose a new dollar bill in it as a token gift. If you desire, write a little message on the back of your card. Copy some scriptures about marriage, such as 1 Corinthians 11:1; 1 Peter 3:7; Ephesians 5:2-33. Say something to them about having a Christian home, and their love for God as their most precious gift they can give each other. Enclose a printed invitation to worship services with times listed if your congregation has this, or just write the times of worship and classes yourself. If enough newlyweds become interested, perhaps your congregation will want to have a special class for newlyweds and how to apply the Bible to their new lives together.

Then there are the baby announcements. They are usually in a little column in a corner of your newspaper somewhere, often the bottom of the page. Send a card to baby and proud parents. They may even put your card in their baby book as the first letter ever received by their child. Tell them how happy you are for them, and what your hopes are for their little one. Tell them that now is the time for them to become a Christian family if they are not yet, so they can be good examples and raise good godly children. If there is a class for new parents on child-rearing the Bible way in your congregation, tell them about it. If there is a class for babies, tell them about this too. Their prospective teacher may wish to follow up your letter with a visit and a little gift such as a bib, a rattle, a picture for baby's room, etc.

You can write to newcomers to your community. This is discussed fully in a separate chapter. But you could have a vital part in this good work. It is so neglected. You could provide the groundwork for this, even while staying home. See how important you are to God's work?

Try to get the birthdays of everyone in your congregation (or divide them up with some other ladies) and send them birthday cards. Your card will in some cases be the only card some people receive on their birthday. This may be a little more expensive if you have a fairly large congregation, and you may wish to ask the church or a career woman in the church to help you with postage.

How far away is the nearest boarding home for the elderly? How many are in your area? How many lonely people does that add up to? You could stay busy just with this one Christian work. It has been years since many people in these homes have received a letter. You know how exciting it is to receive a letter, how you can hardly wait to open the envelope and see what is inside. You feel just a little more loved and wanted after you have received a letter, don't you? Kind of makes you feel warm inside. You can give this same feeling of love to people in senior housing and nursing homes. Use your thinking-of-you cards to begin with, and perhaps you'll want to continue later with some stationery with a scripture verse printed at the top.

What types of things could you write them? You could tell them a little bit about yourself. Perhaps you could select one thing about yourself each time you write, such as the place where you were raised, your occupation or previous occupation, your children, etc. Always try to include God in these letters, such as "That is when I learned from the Bible itself what I must do to be saved," or "I found it very hard/easy to be a Christian when I was in that line of work," or "I have a child who teaches the Bible now," etc. Then ask them about themselves, with specific questions about where they were born, how many in their family, etc.

Talk about the weather, talk about a book you read, talk about your feelings toward God. You could even make one whole letter entirely a prayer for that person. Copy scriptures in your letter that will encourage them. Encourage them in turn to pass on little acts of kindness to those around them. This is especially possible if a person is in senior housing and can get around.

Enclose some stationery and a stamped self-addressed envelope. It is doubtful they have much money. If they cannot answer your letter, perhaps some in the church will visit there and help them with their letter writing, not only to you but also to members of their own family.

On their birthday, perhaps you could send them a Bible game. Everyone loves games. Really. There are quite a few inexpensive ones available. Or you could send them a large-print Bible, or a subscription to a devotional magazine. (More on this in another chapter.)

Do you know of an orphan home or children's home that interests you? Write the administrator and ask for the names of any children who never receive mail, and have no family to take an interest in them. You'll have to change your mood with them, naturally, to a bubbly, happy type letter. They may not answer you as they may not be "letter writers," but you can be guaranteed they will look forward to your cheery letters. Tell them about different children and teenagers in the Bible. They probably don't realize how many teenagers there are in the Bible.

Some of the teenagers listed there were Shem, Ham, and Japheth (born after Noah their father began building the ark); Ishmael (14 when Isaac was born, 17 when sent away from home); Uzziah (16 when became king of Judah); Josiah (19 when led a religious reformation in Judah); Mary, Jesus' mother (most Jewish women married while teenagers); Jesus (12 when went to temple and taught). With further study, you could probably find other teenagers in the Bible.

Very important it is for you to keep yourself available as a listening ear in case the one you are writing to ever needs anyone to confide in. Do not be overly critical of them; there are counselors and personnel there to take care of discipline. Help them from the positive side, with suggestions for good things and good ways to do things.

Do you have any friends with a serviceman or woman stationed away from home? They are lonely - most of them - beyond our understanding. Most have a few fair-weather friends. The principles of Christianity are often absent. These service personnel need a haven of escape, someone to be really interested in them and to understand their daily temptations which are usually many. How hard it is to be a Christian in the military! Write them monthly at least, weekly if possible. Send them some cookies or a good book if you like. Find out when their birthday is for sure. Send them a card, and get all your friends to send them cards too. They may be the only ones they receive.

People who have experienced the death of a parent, child, or mate in the past year, or people who have lost a mate through divorce are in need of friendship and encouragement. The death of a mate is like losing an arm or a leg by amputation because of a terrible accident. It was once a beloved part of that person, and will forever be painfully missed. The loss of a mate through divorce is like losing an arm or leg by amputation because of a cancer that is threatening the rest of the body. Although the amputation of that diseased part may have been necessary, the person was once a beloved active part of them; and the double loss of a mate and that mate's love can be just as devastating.

Those who lose a parent because of death or divorce experience similar pain as the mate left behind, whether they are five or fifty years old. The younger ones especially no longer have someone to ask advice of, to whom they can go to learn how to mature and handle life's difficulties. There seems to be no one out there willing to fill in for these needs, even though the Bible urges at numerous times to take care of the fatherless.

Those who have lost children feel a sense of confused justice: Why did the child have to die before the parent? Thoughts center around "I'd give anything to have died in their place ~ it was my turn and somehow it seems they took my place," and "They were so young and had so much living yet to do." Such painful perplexity leaves feelings of helplessness and possibly guilt over something that cannot be changed.

Write to these people with such terrible losses. Talk to them about God's providence and care; however, do not tell them it was God's will, for God does not desire bad things to happen to anyone, Satan (not God) is the cause of death. Romans 8:28 usually is helpful in that it explains that God can take all things, whether good or bad, and make them work out for good (not necessarily the best, but good) if a person loves God and depends on him in faith for strength.

Mostly offer consolation, knowing that no matter what anyone says, even God, they are going to hurt. Offer love to them. Quote some psalms to them. Tell them about people in the Bible who experienced similar things. Tell them about your having experienced similar things if this is the case. You cannot erase the pain, but you can apply soothing ointment of gentle words.

Do you know someone with a long-term illness, perhaps accompanied with terrible pain, and/or with imminent death? How is this person's faith? During such times, people sometimes begin to question how God could allow bad to happen to them if he loves them. Reassure them that sometimes just the presence of physical pain makes people depressed and think in ways they ordinarily would not. Tell them (if their faith indeed has become weak) that you know their faith will return someday as strong or stronger than ever, and that until then you hope they will cling to your faith to see them through.

Don't forget, in the midst of all this letter writing, to write to your own family members ~ children, parents, nieces, nephews, aunts, uncles, cousins, grandparents. Are any of the young ones in college? If you went to college or even away to camp, share with them your experiences ~ the laughter, the tears, the excitement.

If you are now living alone, write others who are also. Share with them how you have learned to handle it. It takes a special kind of person to live alone and be happy and remain a part of society. Tell them how you do it.

Do you know anyone who became a Christian lately? Write to that person and tell them how you rejoice with God and the angels for them. Copy scriptures on how to stay a Christian. You know, becoming a Christian is one thing, and is probably the easy part. Remaining a Christian from that moment on for years and years is quite another thing, and is full of temptations. Give them ideas on how to be full of Christian works, so they will begin their works immediately. There is no use waiting for them to be older Christians before they start to work. They mature as Christians BY THEIR WORKS. Hebrews 5:13,14 explains this. *For everyone who partakes only of milk is not accustomed to the word of righteousness, for he is a babe. But solid food is for the mature, who BECAUSE OF PRACTICE have their senses trained to discern good and evil.* Help them train their spiritual senses by giving them ideas of ways they can put their Christianity to work.

When people become Christians, they expect their lives to

become different. If they don't become different, they often lose interest and fall away. Older Christians must teach them. As the Ethiopian eunuch said when Philip asked him if he understood what he read, "How can I, unless someone explains it to me?" (Acts 8:31). Help these new Christians grow - show them and teach them -and you too will grow. Write them weekly if you like, showing them scriptures about different phases of the Christian life, just like a weekly lesson at home; and you will be surprised how much you learn yourself in the process.

How many backsliding or backslidden Christians do you know of? When was the last time they attended a Christian assembly? They need you, even though they may not know it yet. Write to them and talk to them about Jesus' sacrifice for them. Talk to them about Hebrews 10:23-27 and our need for each other. Talk to them about eternity. Enclose a tract about *The Day a Church Member Died*, by Thomas Warren, or some similar tract, which your congregation could probably provide for you if needed. Ask why they left. Perhaps no one has done that yet.

Maybe there was some point of doctrine they did not understand. Maybe they were never used in Christian service and did not know what to do on their own. Maybe they got too interested in their favorite sport. Maybe there was someone who said something encouragement took wrong. Be a peacemaker. One of the beatitudes states, *Blessed are the peacemakers, for they will be called sons of God* (Matthew 5:9). Help them make peace between God and themselves. Help them make peace between themselves and their Christian brothers and sisters. Tell them you miss them.

Encourage them to tell you why they left. It very often will be just an excuse, but at least it is a beginning point. And if, by some chance (most will not respond this way) they say they are not interested in the church anymore and wish you'd leave them alone, reassure them that you will continue praying for them and if they ever need anyone, to please contact you. Then try to keep some kind of communication going so you know how their life is going in general. If you ever heard that they are ill, or have come upon bad times, or anything negative occurs in their life, re-establish your correspondence with them; perhaps this time their hearts will be softer. Remember, Romans 8:28 says that God can take anything, whether good or bad, and make it turn into something good for a person who loves him. Perhaps you could help them look to God in their time of adversity, possibly the only time they would even consider thinking about God, and help them return to him. But never give up on them.

There is one other group of people who discontinue attending worship services for a reason most would never think about. People going through a great deal of trauma in their lives have their emotions right next to the surface all the time. They can keep their emotions under control at work and other such gatherings. But they cannot keep them under control during a worship service, especially during the singing. So, remember, just because someone has quit attending, it does not necessarily mean they do not wish to attend. They may be at a breaking point and believe they would reach it if they attended and bared their souls in worship. Write these people gentle letters, and tell them you would like to sit with them in church if they'll come back.

Have you ever thought of encouraging your own elders, deacons, teachers, and ministers? The elders, especially, are holding a great burden, for they are ever watching over your souls, as those who will give an account. Let them do this with joy and not with grief, for this would be unprofitable for you (Hebrews 13:17).

It is not easy being an elder. It is not easy being in a position to have to give account of all the souls he is put over, as an elder is. He is responsible for you and the others within your congregation. Sometimes he tries to talk to someone to help them learn to stay away from unwise company or unwise deeds, and that person may turn on him instead of realizing he is trying to help and guide him as a father. Then there are the decisions about personal work programs, missionary work, benevolent work. Trying to keep any kind of organization functioning properly (remember, the church is an organization too - a spiritual one) takes time and stamina.

Elders have feelings, and they get discouraged sometimes. They may never show it in front of you, but it happens. Write to them occasionally and tell them how much you appreciate them. This may be exactly what your elders need right now. Don't overlook them by thinking they are superhuman. They are not. They need encouragement the same way that you do at times, and we all do. All of the leaders of the church can be given a boost by a special "thank you" letter or note from you.

You could even do personal work from your home to bring people to Christ. Often a local congregation advertises Bible correspondence courses in the newspaper along with its listing of services. Help with this work.

Many foreign missionaries advertise Bible correspondence courses in their local newspapers. Many hundreds of thousands of people have written in for such courses. Do you know the language of the people where such courses are being offered? Write the missionary there and offer to assist in grading them.

But you do not have to know foreign languages to help with foreign missionary work. Some American congregations have run correspondence courses in English-language newspapers overseas very successfully. Help with this. Write a letter. Save a soul.

What about the destiny of these nations and of our own nation? 1 Timothy 2:1-4 exhorts us specifically in this regard: *I urge then, first of all, that requests, prayer, intercession and thanksgiving be made for everyone - for kings and all those in authority, that we may live peaceful and quiet lives in all godliness and holiness. This is good, and pleases God our Savior who wants all men to be saved and to come to a knowledge of the truth.*

Send a brief message to our president, our senators, our government officials ~ even those of other nations. They have the destiny of our nation, indeed our whole world, in their hands. They need God's guidance. Write them a note and tell them you are praying for them. They will appreciate this. You may or may not agree with all they stand for, but *the prayer of a righteous man is powerful and effective* (James 5:16b).

You can even write a letter to the world. You can write a book. If you feel you have found the "secret" to applying a certain part of Christianity to your life, write about it. Write it in the form of a story or documentary or lesson. If you haven't enough material for a book, write an article and send it to a Christian magazine. They may be interested in what you have to say. Write a poem, if that is your gift. Put it to music if you like; we need more Christian songs.

There is so much you can do for your Lord with pen and paper. You do not ever have to say, "There is nothing for me to do, because I can't get out and go anywhere." There is something for you - a great deal more than you alone could ever handle. Your possibilities of Christian service are limitless with just this one tool ~ a pen. When you finish this chapter, sit down and write a letter to someone right then. If you do not have money for postage and envelopes, tell the church. They may help you. Or an individual class may, or a career woman in your congregation. Write as many letters as you can, and feel the warmth of having served swell up within you. You will be so blessed for it. And most of all, Christ and his church will be glorified.

3 ~ BENEVOLENCE

The word benevolent comes from the Old French word *bene*, meaning well, and *volens*, meaning to wish. In other words, it means to wish well. Today it means more than just the wish, but also the very act of helping someone get along well. We usually think of benevolence as involving material things.

Benevolence is referred to in the Bible usually in regard to widows and orphans, for they had no way of supporting themselves; and often today they do not either. The handicapped in Bible times had no source of income except alms. The aged had no source of income. Everyone had to depend on relatives or friends ~ if indeed they had any. They certainly had no government welfare programs except for limited help from the temple tax.

It seems that the poor then were treated much like the poor of today, for truly human nature throughout the ages never changes. Leviticus 25:35-37 refers to the abomination of loaning money to the poor for high interest (usury). If the poor spoke out against his oppression, or even spoke out for any cause, Ecclesiastes 9:13 says that he was either forgotten or unnoticed in the first place. Proverbs 14:20 states that the poor are resented and looked down on. Even in the new Christian era James admonished the saints for leaving the poor standing in the back of their assemblies and bringing the rich to the forefront (James 2:2-4), and this is still done today.

Webster defines affliction as distress, calamity, misfortune. Job 34:28 says that these afflicted ones cry out due to their misfortunes. Oppression is defined in the dictionary as a heavy weight on the mind, a burden, being trampled on, being kept down by cruel or unjust use of power.

Job 20:19 contends that the oppressed are forsaken, for their houses are taken from them. Psalm 12:5 refers to the oppressed as sighing, and Psalm 74:2 states that they are shameful. Therefore, society brings the poor down to a low estate (Psalm 109:39), and judgment and justice toward them is perverted in favor of the rich and powerful (Ecclesiastes 5:9).

Because of all this, the poor usually have a very poor frame of mind, poor attitudes. Isaiah 14:3 explains that the poor are full of fear and sorrow. Proverbs 1:27 relates that the poor are full of fear, distress, and anguish. But often these same poor try to cover up their fears, and it all comes out as anger (Psalm 90:11) and fighting (Song of Solomon 3:8).

If they have been in such a state for very many years, they will be in a mental attitude of, "What's the use of trying? Society has done this to me, so why shouldn't I get as much back from society as I can any way I can? Besides, I'll never been any different; society will make sure of that too. Just why should I even try anymore?"

Now society may not have created the first cause of this poverty, but society often could do something to help them out of their calamity. If this help (applied properly) does not come swiftly after the calamity, a feeling of hopelessness enters the mind of the poor and could remain there until death.

The Bible does tell us how to help the poor overcome this fear within themselves, which is the first step toward getting out of this way of life. 1 John 4:18 tells us to love them. Luke 6:36,38 tells us to have mercy, to not judge them, to not condemn them, and to give them their necessities. Romans 12:16 commands us to condescend to men of low estate. And 1 Corinthians 10:12 warns us to take heed lest we too fall.

There are several ways we can help the poor overcome the outside forces of society that seem to gang up on them and keep them in a state of helplessness and a feeling of selflessness. Psalm 12:51 tells us we can rescue them from the puffed up, those who degrade the poor. Psalm 82:3-5 tells us we can defend them and make sure they receive justice. And Psalm 22:23,24 says we should not give in to society's demands that we abhor the poor.

However, in the process of helping the poor in these ways, we should be most careful to not fall into the trap of the "Rescue Triangle." This triangle consists of two people ~ a rescuer, a victim, and later on a switching of roles to that of persecutor/rejecter.

The RESCUER is a person who feels the need to do things for others. They glean their sense of worthwhileness from relationships with people who they view as powerless. They assume responsibility for other people, deal with other people's problems for them, and make decisions for them. Sometimes people become so-called rescuers unintentionally when a victim manipulates them by acting more helpless than they really are and making the rescuer not want to hurt their feelings.

The VICTIM is a person who feels helpless to have any control over what makes them happy or any other part of their life. They blame others for their problems and have a ton of reasons/excuses for why they are not happy. They not only blame others, but they also expect others to solve their problems for them; they claim no responsibility for what has happened to them or for dealing with it after it happens.

The PERSECUTOR is a person who is angry, hurt and frustrated and unleashes these feelings on other people, usually by means of severe criticism. They see these feelings as being other people's fault and so they persecute in revenge. Both rescuer and victim can switch to the persecutor role at any time.

How is the game played?

The victim does not use all their power to overcome their problems. The rescuer does not encourage them to do so, but rather takes all the responsibility and makes all the decisions. The rescuer sees herself as a powerful person in comparison to the victim and feels "holier than thou." The rescuer/victim relationship continues as long as both sides cooperate, the victim refusing to take responsibility and the rescuer willing to take it all. Until....

The victim doesn't seem to get any better. Usually the victim does not follow through or live up to some decision the rescuer made for them. So the rescuer gets angry and becomes the persecutor. They have done all this hard work and there is no pay-off. Both sides become tired, angry and upset. The victim responds to the persecution, often by switching roles to become the persecutor herself. In the final scene, both people feel worse and blame each other for their failure.

No one enjoys feeling inferior to other people or helpless or miserable. And the feeling is made even worse by people who agree with one's powerlessness by a so-called rescue. No matter how weak we feel, it is good to hear that we are not completely powerless and are expected to do our own part by someone who is willing to help.

Most of us have worked enthusiastically in behalf of people who eventually proved to have been not only disinterested in our help, but actually disdainful of it. Most of us have, after working hard with a person and having no success, gotten angry and subtly or overtly persecuted the person. There are four things to keep in mind to avoid the "Rescue Triangle:"

[1] For true help to take place, the person needing help must be seen as a complete human being capable of having power over their own life. [2] Both the helper and the helped need to understand themselves and be clear on what to expect from each other. [3] Each must consider what they are willing to do and then agree together on whatever action will be taken. [4] All the power that is available to the person being helped must be used. Whenever efforts are unequal, the relationship is unequal. There must be a balance and equality. In such a relationship you will be a true helper.

Of course we should never help others for the reward of people. If people reward us, God will not (Matthew 6:2), and that's a fact! On the other hand, our rewards from God for helping those in some kind of need are many. Deuteronomy 15:7-11 says that if you will open wide your hand toward the poor, you will be blessed by God in all your works and in all you put your hand to do. Daniel 4:27 says that if you show mercy to the poor, your tranquility will be lengthened. And finally, Matthew 25:44-46 says that if you do these things, you will have life eternal.

Then the righteous will answer him, "Lord, when did we see you hungry and feed you, or thirsty and give you something to drink? When did we see you a stranger and invite you in, or needing clothes and clothe you? When did we see you sick or in prison and go to visit you?" The King will reply, "I tell you the truth, whatever you did for one of the least of these brothers of mine, you did for me" (Matthew 25:37-40).

Let us first consider the hungry. We do not have as many hungry in America as we used to. During the Depression, people went from door to door asking if someone would give them a meal to eat on the back porch. We have government programs now, and "soup kitchens" and food stamps, Meals on Wheels, etc. But there are some people out there with much pride and they refuse to accept what they consider "handouts." These are very often older people who feel a great need to keep their dignity. Even if you go to their home with cans of food, they are likely to tell you they are getting along fine without any help.

If such is the case, perhaps your best bet would be to invite them to your home for a hot and highly nutritious meal as often as possible - perhaps once a week. Or, perhaps there is something that these people have they no longer use which you could request to buy or trade for some groceries. Another way you may be able to do it is to leave a little money at their grocery store anonymously if they are known by the clerk or manager.

Also, you could help their grocery fund by providing transportation to the store and doctor so they do not have to spend their limited funds on taxis and bus. You could also have potluck dinners for them to come to where they bring one inexpensive dish such as gelatins, but have access to more expensive and nutritious food brought by others.

Families are burned out more often than we sometimes realize. Be ready for these families when it happens. Collect cans of food and other imperishable foods, save several sizes of clothing and shoes as well as linens, and keep in mind the furniture and dishes you have that you could lend or share in time of such need. Be ready for the calamity before it happens, for fires destroy everything immediately and the need is immediate. At such times there is little time to go around collecting.

Another catastrophe that hits some around us which we often do not even think to check out is inconceivably high medical bills. Sometimes even if someone has medical insurance, the bills go far beyond what is payable by the insurance company or Medicaid either one. In order to meet these expenses, the family often has to mortgage the home or refinance it, sell their car, cut down on food and clothing, get extra jobs, and borrow from banks at high interest. Yet many families will never say a word about this to anyone.

Do go to them as a friend and try to get them to level with you if you are close to them. If they need help but do not want to accept it, explain to them that It is more blessed to give than to receive (Acts 20:35) if that will help any. Then tell them that someday, after they are out of this difficulty, they will no doubt run across someone else who needs the same kind of help and they can best repay you by passing the gesture on to them.

As with food, most people are not without clothing. However, there are those who do need help with this. If you do not know of anyone, you may contact a nursing home, a state hospital, a veterans' hospital, or home for severely handicapped children. Some of the people in such institutions have no family to come see them, and very low income with which to buy clothing. It is surprising how few clothes some of them have. You or a group with which you are affiliated may wish to "adopt" a man and woman, or boy and girl. Send them a little something each spring and fall. They wouldn't wear out their clothes very fast so wouldn't need much; but they do need some. Make or purchase for them new clothes if possible.

You may wish to have a special clothes closet and notify the public schools in your area that they are available for any children needing clothes. If there are sales on tennis shoes or boots occasionally in the stores for a fraction of the regular cost, buy several and keep them on hand. School children seem always to be needing shoes and socks.

Your congregation's clothes closet may be used by new people who wish to attend Bible classes but are embarrassed by their clothes. Of course we know they would be accepted no matter what they wore, but people do want to wear the best possible when they go to worship their King, so be prepared to help them.

For this purpose, have some suits on hand that are in good condition, some shirts, some ties, some pretty dresses. Put sizes on them and hang them up neatly with hangers on a rack (no cardboard boxes, please!). Make the room the clothes are in, regardless of size, have a little dignity to it. If large enough, make it look more like a shop than an attic. Let the people who obtain clothing in this way keep a little of their self-respect. Hang a mirror on the door, put a little rug on the floor, and if there's room, put a picture or two on the wall.

What can you do for the sick? They may be only down with a cold or be lying down on the sofa watching television. But still they are not feeling well and probably have more miseries (blowing, coughing, sniffling, etc.) than some with more serious illnesses. So, regardless of their ailment and the duration of it, they need a little help.

When you arrive, wander into the kitchen for a drink of water. You'll probably find dishes sitting in the sink. Roll up your sleeves and tell the person you'll put their dishes in some soapy water or dishwasher or wash them up for them, depending on the habit of the person you are helping. If they protest, tell them you will be ill someday, and then they can come over and you'd be most happy for them to do your dishes for them! (Say it with a big smile of course.)

Then go into the bathroom, and on your way see if the beds are made. If they're not, quietly make them, or at least throw the bedspread up over the pillows (again, whatever that person ordinarily does). If the person protests to this, just say that it just took a few minutes and wasn't any trouble for such a special friend. Then sit down with them for a short conversation, mixed with a little humor. Remember Proverbs 17:22, *A merry heart is good medicine.* Before you leave, have a short prayer for them, naming them by name. And on your way out the door, ask if there's anything they need at the drug store.

If the person who is sick has an illness that is going to last longer than a few days, tell them you would like to come in a couple times a week to tidy up for them. And if such is the case, remind them of all the times they have helped other people, and this is God's way of repaying that help. Once a week you may wish to take home a bundle of laundry or throw it in their washer and dryer.

Whenever you return, bring a casserole for the family to eat, especially if the wife is the one who is ill or busy taking care of the sick one. You might include a card with the recipe as a way of saying, "I know you could have cooked this if you'd had a chance." Or you might say you just discovered a new recipe and would like their opinion on it (if that's the case). Anything to help them see you're not seeing them as a "charity case." Be sure to return for the empty dish so they won't have the responsibility of remembering who it belongs to and then carrying it around in the car until they see you. Better yet, put your food in disposable dishes.

Another thing you can do for someone who is ill for any length of time is to write letters for them. Also, you could read to them from the Bible or a devotional book. Help them get their bills paid by mailing them or delivering them yourself, whichever is most convenient for you. Tape each Sunday's sermons and lend the tape to them each week. Of course, send them cards now and then. If their illness will keep them in bed for perhaps years, several people could go together to buy them the New Testament on tapes or CDs.

If you know of anyone in the hospital who needs blood, please do help them in this way if you can. Blood costs over $100 per pint. Even if you do not have the same blood type, you can donate in that person's name and your blood will be put in the blood bank in place of that which is used in the patient's type. What a noble gift -the gift of life!

You may wish to contact a local hospital to see if you can make favors to go on the trays every Sunday morning. The dietitian is usually the one to talk to, as her staff would be the ones putting the favors on the trays. You could choose four different types of favors and repeat them each month since most people are not in the hospital any longer than that. Be sure to include Bible verses on all your favors. Never miss an opportunity to encourage. Offer a Bible correspondence course to do during their convalescing days. Your little tray gifts will be wonderful visitors for them on the Lord's day.

Remember Jesus went about healing people. This is what he did to prove God's love for them, and to prove he was the Son of God. Once he did this, they were anxious to learn more about him, anxious to be with him and to be like him. By helping the sick, you can attract people to Jesus' love the same way, and then they will want to learn more about the One who inspired you to be so loving. They will know more of what it means that God is Love through you. Through you ~ also God's child ~ they will be able to know his love for them.

Now let us consider what we can do for those in prison. This is a little more difficult. People in prison are often bitter, either over what they did or for getting caught. Those bitter for getting caught are nearly impossible to help. Those bitter over what they did and are sorry for it are easier to help, but can be hard to convince when you do want to help them. The atmosphere in prisons is not the best, as it is usually filled with resentment, for naturally no one wants to be there.

There are some in prison who do wish someone really cared about what happens to them, and whether or not they live or die. You could write to the chaplain or warden of a prison and ask if you could send him some letters for him to pass on to anyone who does not have correspondents on the "outside." You may receive only one person's name. That is enough for a beginning. If you really become a help to them and a boost to their morale, they will pass the word on.

Tell them a little about yourself. If you ever had anyone in your family or among your acquaintances who was ever in prison, tell them so, and they will feel that you might understand them a little better. Ask them how long they are to serve and if they have in mind any certain type of occupation when they get out. Ask if they are in any vocational or other educational programs in the prison, including college. Ask about their family ~ where they live, how they are getting along. Offer to write to the family too, if you can have their address.

Just remember that all your mail will be read before given to the prisoner, and that the prisoner's mail will be read by a prison official before being mailed to you. Also, there are only certain days they can send out mail, and only certain people they are permitted to write. One very important thing you will want to do is ask them if they would like to study the Bible with you by mail. You might be surprised at their eagerness to do so. Remember, the thing they have the most of is time ~ time to kill or time to come alive.

A classic example of a "hardened criminal" eventually being helped to see Christ's love for him is Clyde V. Thompson, at one time the "meanest man in Texas prisons." His book, *Clyde Thompson EX 83*, Tells about his having killed four men, led prison riots, wounded prison guards, and being sentenced to be executed. Then someone came to visit him in prison. This changed his whole life. He finally had some meaning in it. He turned to his loving Savior and was baptized into Christ.

He began excitedly teaching his fellow inmates and baptizing them at an average rate of one a day. He also wrote, *The Best Way Out is Up* published by Star Publishing Company in Fort Worth, Texas, and numerous tracts including *I was Sentenced to Death in the Electric Chair*, and *What is Freedom?* also published by Star. These tracts were written for prisoners. The chaplain of a prison could tell you if there is a prison ministry you could become a part of. They could certainly give you further advice on how to handle various situations with anyone you are communicating with. Do keep in mind that you must obey all prison rules; don't ever try to go around them.

If the prisoner you write to has a family living near you, go see them and become their friend. Doubtless they have few true friends at this time if it is known about their prisoner relative. Encourage them and help them. Help them make the best of now and use now to prepare for a good future. Help them keep up their hopes. Teach them the same things you are teaching the prisoner so that their faith can grow together.

And if your prisoner is going to be paroled in the near future, someone on the outside will be needed to help line up a job, for they cannot be paroled without a job arranged for ahead of time. Be a spokesman in the community. Whatever that person does well, find a company that deals in that and make some phone calls. Consult the phone book as well as want ads. Contact the state employment office, or go over there to the office yourself and go through their microfiche or computer listings of job available. Level with the people you talk to and tell them he is coming out of prison soon and wants to do this type work. Tell them he has a family ~ if indeed he has one. Answer any questions as truthfully as you know how. You will find surprisingly many people willing to give him a break toward a new and better life.

If the family does not plan to live in the same location after release, help them find a place to live. Moving to another area helps break ties with old so-called friends who also get into trouble with the law. One of the most important necessities of living a "clean life" is to stay away from old friends and influences, and make new friends with good influences. Psalm 1:1, Proverbs 13:20 and 1 Corinthians 15:33 tell about this. Keep in mind, however, that they probably feel very uncomfortable with "good people" as they probably think "good people" do not think of them as "good."

Be sure to keep in mind while working with prisoners the "Rescue Triangle" discussed earlier. This type of activity is a way of life with most of them. They feel victimized by society, so they persecute society, then society punishes them. Thus they feel victimized again. It is the victim stage that they are in while in prison. Extreme care must be taken to build them up and tell them they are a worthwhile individual capable of having a fulfilling and peaceful life as a result of their own efforts.

Those who return to prison are those who get frustrated after their release because society seemingly hasn't made their life any better. So they return to their old ways, and persecuting society and are punished again (return to the victim stage). Only feeling the love of God can change them, and being convinced, "I can do everything through him who gives me strength" (Philippians 4:13). You cannot change a prisoner's attitude and destiny ~ only God can do that.

Yes, there is much you could do to help prisoners and ex-convicts get a new start. Indeed, you could make the difference in whether or not someone makes it for good or turns right around and ends up in prison again. Just remember, all have sinned and fall short of the glory of God (Romans 3:23).

Another way you could show benevolence is to take a foster child into your home. Usually such a child has a family with many problems, more than they can cope with. As a result, they cannot communicate with their children in a warm and understanding way. In some instances, the foster child has both parents in the hospital at the same time, or some similar situation. But usually a child needs a home because of emotional problems among the family members or with the parents, such as alcoholism, unemployment, etc.

Regardless of the reason, these children need to know they are wanted and loved and even needed. Touch a child's life with yours. It may be for only a few days during a brief family crisis. Or it may be for many months. But the blessing will last forever.

You may wish to help an unmarried girl who is pregnant and needs somewhere to live away from her home town in order to avert the shame she might ordinarily feel among her friends. These girls are frightened and disillusioned. Things did not turn out for them as they had expected. What is life all about anyway? They sought love and ended up hating themselves even more. Show them people do care for them and love them in a very special way, regardless of the direction their life has turned. Show them that they can get back up after they stumble, and they can continue their walk through life with confidence from above and from within.

In keeping foster children or unwed expectant mothers, apply to the social service agency dealing with adoptions and foster homes to become licensed. This is not as complicated as it may seem, but is a necessity. There are several Christian agencies scattered among the larger cities of our nation. You will need room enough to care for these people, which will involve a home visit for verification. Also the home visit will give the officials some ideas of your home life. You will need to give several references and a general personal background. In some states you need not be married to help with these people temporarily without a home. You will likely receive a little monetary assistance from the agency to help support the child, but not much.

Probably the most long-standing way you can help someone in need is to adopt a baby or a child. Getting approval to adopt is similar to getting a license as a foster parent. Probably the main difference is that in most states you must prove you cannot have children yourself. However, this is not a law in all states anymore. The other difference is that you must pay a lawyer's fee and, if a baby is involved, the hospital bill.

If you feel the wait is too long, you could consider adopting a baby from a country having economic problems such as Eastern Europe or South America. In that case, you should go to the country you are interested in, locate where the orphanages are, and contact a local attorney. Once you have done that, you need to contact the U.S. Department of Naturalization and Immigration and an American attorney. You will have to satisfy the laws of two countries. Do be sure to thoroughly check the health of the child you wish to adopt.

If you cannot adopt a child but do live near a children's home, "adopt" a child or two or three on weekends. Give them a chance to live in a "normal" house with a few brothers and sisters and a pet if you have one. Give them a chance to have individual attention, rather than feeling lost in a small crowd. They probably receive as much love and attention in their place of residence as possible, considering there are usually a much larger number of "brothers and sisters" per house parent than in private homes. But they could always use more love and more attention from you, their second parents. Take them somewhere special on their birthday and other holidays. Send them to camp.

We also have the homeless. It seems that, as the divorce rate rose, so did the homeless rate. Of course it is always bad during high unemployment times too. We'd had the problem during the Depression, but thought it was overcome now. It wasn't. Stock-market near crashes have occurred since, putting many out of work.

There are soup kitchens and there are temporary overnight shelters. But these people need permanent homes. Some would not keep a job and you cannot help them with a house yet ~ that is too premature for their other problems. But, if you would like to help a homeless family, you can contact lending organizations, the Department of Housing and Urban Renewal, and the Veterans Administration to get a list of housing that has been repossessed. Sometimes such properties can be purchased for just a few thousand dollars. You can get a group of people together to go in and fix the house up. Then, if not personally know a homeless family you can notify your state's Department of Social Services or even Habitat for Humanity to see if there is a reliable homeless family who needs the house.

There is a lot in this one chapter to choose from. Anyone could keep you busy indefinitely. God guide you as you make your selection.

4 ~ HANDICAPPED

What does a handicap mean? It is indeed probably not the first thing you think of. The *Britannica World Language Dictionary* gives as its first definition, "*A condition imposed to equalize the chances of competitors in a race or athletic contest, as the carrying of extra weight, or the requirement of a greater distance or a later start than is assigned to an inferior competitor.*"

Perhaps God saw special spiritual and mental capabilities in some people, and felt they needed a handicap in this race of life to keep them fairly equal to the rest of the human race. If this is true, we had better take a better look at the "handicapped" people we know!

The apostle Paul had a handicap. In 2 Corinthians 12:7 he explained, *And lest I should be exalted above measure, through the abundance of the revelations, there was given to me a thorn in the flesh, the messenger of Satan to buffet me, lest I should be exalted above measure* (KJV). He also spoke of people's reaction to him in person, *for his letters, say they, are weighty and powerful: but his bodily presence is weak, and his speech contemptible* (2 Corinthians 10:10, KJV).

Who were some of the other handicapped people found in the Bible? Surprisingly, many of them were spiritual leaders of their day.

There were blind people. Isaac, the promised son of Abraham and father of Israel (Genesis 48:10) was one. Eli, high priest and judge of the Israelites, and teacher of the prophet Samuel (1 Samuel 4:15) was another. Ahijah, a prophet of God (1 Kings 14:4) was yet another. And of course the apostle Paul was temporarily blind (Acts 9:8-19).

What can we do for the blind today? Our society is pretty much accepting of the blind. Our egos do not feel threatened when we are around them. And there are various programs set up to help them get along in their own homes.

Can they read Braille? If they cannot, ask if they would like to, and contact your local library for information on where to go to learn. Once they do know how to read Braille, help them get a Braille Bible as well as other books and magazines in Braille. Records and tapes of the Bible and other materials are also available from the library. If you and some friends could go together to present a blind person with a Bible they can use, that would be a wonderful gift.

Do they need transportation? Some blind people are comfortable walking around town with their white cane and/or seeing-eye dog; and they should not be discouraged from doing this. Who doesn't enjoy their independence? But there will be times that they need a ride to someplace too far to walk or too inconvenient: Doctor's office, grocery store, church, library, etc. They go to pretty much the same type places you do.

Include them in social functions. They enjoy music, so if you go to a concert, invite them along. There might be a play they are interested in. Include them in parties of sighted people their age. Ask them to come early so you can show them where everything will be and they can become familiar and comfortable.

If they like to correspond with people, help them learn to type. They can write letters and stay in touch with friends this way. There are computer programs out for the blind now which use voice synthesizing. There is some public domain software along this line that costs only about $10. Look through the ads of a computer magazine for one of the public-domain software catalogs. They can write letters and stay in touch with friends this way. Or they may be talented writers, and should be encouraged to write articles and books. The world will never have too many books.

Make sure their telephone is usable and practical for them. Call them every day to see how they're doing. Encourage them to use the telephone for their own good works. There are people in the community who need someone to call them every day to see how they are doing; primarily the elderly and handicapped. They could also use the telephone to call people who are sick or have other problems so they can encourage them, and even pray for them while they're on the line. Yes, there are some special good works that people who are blind can do. After all, it didn't stop people in Bible times, and it needn't stop blind people today either.

In addition to the blind, there are people who are hearing impaired. The Bible does not mention any such people by name, but it does mention their needs. Leviticus 19:14 says: *Do not curse the deaf or put a stumbling block in front of the blind, but fear your God.* And we have a beautiful account of Jesus helping someone who was deaf in Mark 7:32-37.

> *There some people brought a man to him who was deaf and could hardly talk, and they begged him to place his hand on the man. After he took him aside, away from the crowd, Jesus put his fingers into the man's ears. Then he spit and touched the man's tongue. He looked up to heaven and with a deep sigh said to him, "Ephphatha!" (which means, "Be opened!"). At this, the man's ears were opened, his tongue was loosened and he began to speak plainly. Jesus commanded them not to tell anyone. But the more he did so, the more they kept talking about it. People were overwhelmed with amazement. "He has done everything well," they said. "He even makes the deaf hear and the dumb speak."*

What can you do for the deaf? Keep in mind that since they cannot hear, they cannot hear their own speech and therefore it is often unclear. The first thing you can do for them is learn to communicate with them. It is fun making up your own sign language, just as you would with someone who speaks another spoken language. But eventually, if you are with them very much, you need to learn their language. They will help you, if you like, and in the process you will become good friends.

Without hearing, they often cannot get a driver's license. They need transportation. This is a great service to them. You can also act as an interpreter for business transactions such as at the bank, in stores, etc.

Do they belong to groups that have other deaf people in them? Help them locate such groups or organize one. People with similar problems like to get together to encourage each other, exchange ideas, and just have fun while using their own methods of communicating.

Are they able to worship? If they go to a service for only the hearing, they are missing the singing and praying and sermon. But this does not have to be. You could start out with just one, and sit next to that person, perhaps in a side aisle so you can see the worship leaders and your friend both. Then you could "sign" the service for them. Advertise this in the newspaper and with organizations in town who work with the deaf, offering to provide transportation. Then as the group gets a little larger, you will have to stand in front of them to "sign" so they will all be able to see you. What a marvelous Christian service this would be to them! The rewards would be many.

What can the deaf do to serve others? Let me speak directly to these special people. You who are deaf can help prepare Bible school materials for teachers. You can help with Bible correspondence courses. Although you probably could not teach in person, you could help write special Bible lessons for various classes. You could visit nursing homes and senior boarding homes, giving a note to each person you visit saying, "I cannot hear you, but I wanted to let you know I love you." Then you could give them a big hug and a big smile. You could help with little children's classes since the younger children need shown more than told how to do things anyway. There is much the deaf can do just by looking around for opportunities.

Then there are those who cannot walk and must rely on wheelchairs. (There is a special chapter for these who must remain in bed, the chapter on prayer.) Jonathan, son of King Saul, and King David's closest friend, had a son who was lame, named Mephibosheth. He was dropped by his nurse as a baby and both feet were injured. Apparently he had continual pain and problems with his feet throughout life, for many years later when David had grown children, it is said that Mephibosheth went through a period of mourning and not taking care of his feet (2 Samuel 4:4; 19:24).

In Jesus' day, people who would today be confined to wheelchairs were carried around on mats by their friends and relatives. We have accounts of Jesus, Philip, and Peter healing such people who were called "palsied." One such occasion is related in Matthew 8:5,6,13:

When Jesus had entered Capernaum, a centurion came to him, asking for help. "Lord," he said, "my servant lies at home paralyzed and in terrible suffering." Then Jesus said to the centurion, "Go! It will be done just as you believed it would." And his servant was healed at that very hour.

Let's talk about those who are confined to wheelchairs. There are many types of people like this. If their legs are not used at all, eventually they atrophy. Such people usually keep their legs covered in public in order to avoid embarrassing anyone who finds this awkward. In some instances, they were born without proper use of legs or arms either.

Perhaps they have a form of palsy in which movement is made impossible or uncontrolled.

Of those in wheelchairs, probably the hardest for us to feel comfortable around are those who cannot control the movement of most of their body, nor of their facial muscles. It is difficult for us to see them as intelligent human beings; but in many cases, this is the fact. Since they do not fit our stereotype of the "intelligent" person, we need to get to know them better in order to get past that notion.

At first you may feel many emotions: Fright, anger, embarrassment, pity. So prepare yourself ahead of time. You can learn about others who have been able to accomplish good things in this world despite their handicap. There are those who "run" in marathon races; they may come in last, but they run. At this writing, the most intelligent person in the world since Einstein is such a person, a physicist in England. These are the types of things you need to learn so you can quit pitying them and begin admiring them. Contact your local Easter Seals chapter, a veterans' hospital, a rehabilitation center, or any other organization that works with the crippled. You will hear stories of courageous conquerors.

There may be someone in particular that you would like to help, perhaps someone you have seen attend worship with your congregation, or someone down the street, or the relative of a friend. If this person cannot talk clearly, you need to learn about that person through their relatives. Tell them you'd like to start spending some time with them, and it will help you if you know what their interests are, what their aspirations are, what their past accomplishments have been. Then you are ready to approach that person

When you first meet, tell them you'd like to become friends. (Don't say, "I want to become your friend." That sounds condescending.) Tell them you'd like to spend time together sometimes.

If you cannot understand them when they speak, tell them you'd like to learn to understand them using whatever method they have found most successful. This means you will have to take time to learn their method. Just be as patient with yourself as they will be with you. And while you are learning to communicate by word, you can also communicate with touch, a smile, reading to them, taking them for "strolls" outside, and so on.

If they have an electric typewriter or computer, perhaps that could be a source of communication. If they do not have one, ask if they'd like to learn to type (even if it is with a stick between two fingers or their teeth). Then try to locate a typewriter or computer for them.

If the person's speech is not affected, of course you will begin communicating by word immediately. Tell them you heard they wanted to start doing such and such, and have already started doing such and such. Ask them to tell you about these activities. They will be most happy to. It is sometimes difficult for them to find anyone who will take them seriously enough to have an intelligent conversation. Since they can do little else, the use of their intellect often becomes quite refined and they bypass their peers intellectually.

Ask to see samples of what they have done. Then ask them what you can do to help them do even more. It may be they want to learn to play the piano, or go to college, or become a teacher, or any number of things. Whatever it is, assure them that hey can accomplish it, and together you will reach that goal. Someday, somehow, it will be done. Do they have the physical capabilities to drive but don't have their license? Go to the Department of Motor Vehicles and ask what the requirements are. Then help this person make adjustments in a car or van and learn to drive so they can get their license and become more independent.

If they cannot get a license, offer transportation for them. If you have a van, that is one good way to handle it If you cannot fill this need personally, check around until you can find appropriate transportation for them. They may need transportation to physical therapy, the store, a friend's house. And of course they would like the opportunity to attend worship somewhere. Take them with you if at all possible.

If the person is able to live in their own home, try to arrange for physical adjustments such as wider doors, a roll-in shower, lower cabinets, outside ramps, etc. if they are still without them.

This person may wish to develop a vocation. Help them get in touch with any training institutions in the area that offer what they need.

It may mean learning to work on an assembly line, repairing things, becoming a secretary, becoming a college professor. Whatever it is, you could help them accomplish this.

Do they have friends in a similar situation? Introduce some of them by phone if they do not. Then try to get them together for occasional visits. As they get to know a few others, plan a party with them. They need each other's company for mutual support.

And in the midst of helping them, if there is anything they can do for you, let them know. They will be developing a friendship with you, and as the old saying goes, "What are friends for?". So let them be a friend to you too.

Yes, you can help these people with physical handicaps. They are intelligent and courageous human beings and want opportunities to have a fulfilling life and happy eternity, just like everyone else does. Helping them be independent and accomplish as many of their life goals as possible is the greatest thing in the world you could do for them.

Now we will discuss a different kind of handicapped person. This person may be an adult and have a strong, healthy body. But their intellect perhaps has been handicapped so that they still reason like children.

Jesus said many years ago, *Believe me, unless you change your whole outlook and become like little children you will never enter the kingdom of Heaven. It is the man who can be as humble as this little child who is greatest in the kingdom of Heaven. Anyone who welcomes one child like this for my sake is welcoming me* (Matthew 18:2-5, Phillips Version).

God makes a distinction between the thinking processes of children and adults. Paul encouraged, *My brothers, don't be like excitable children but use your intelligence! By all means be innocent as babes as far as evil is concerned, but where your minds are concerned be full-grown men* (1 Corinthians 14:20, Phillips Version).

It just may well be that God felt adults needed reminders of child-like attitudes from more than just children. It just could be that God gives us what we call "mentally handicapped" adults so we could see child-like innocence, wonder, and acceptance in a grown body. Let us, therefore, re-examine our feelings toward these special people.

When in their COMPASSION they cry upon learning of someone else's misfortune, do we think they're going too far? When their GRACE allows them to be friends with someone others dislike, do we wonder where their sense of pride is? When someone makes a cutting remark to them and being so SLOW TO ANGER, they just smile in innocent response, do we wonder why they can't take a hint? When their LOVE FLOWS out so freely and unashamedly that they think nothing of giving others a hug right in public, do you think they ought to be more modest? When someone tells them to go away, yet later they return because of loyalty and FAITHFULNESS, do you wonder what keeps them coming back? And when people make fun of them or mistakenly call them idiots or morons, and they FORGIVE them time and again, do you wonder if they're missing the point? You do not have to wonder about these things, for these special people are just REFLECTING THE GLORY OF GOD.

Just what is God's glory? Moses asked this same question when he asked to see God. And when God passed in front of Moses, he revealed that his glory was COMPASSION, GRACE, SLOWNESS TO ANGER, ABOUNDING LOVE, FAITHFULNESS, AND FORGIVENESS (Exodus 33:18-34:7).

Indeed, these special people whom we call mentally handicapped are God's special gift to show us more clearly his glory. The person whose intellect has been slowed down is free to concentrate on the emotions and thus more easily reflect godly attitudes, just as a little child does.

An unknown author wrote an article entitled, A CHILD SHALL LEAD, and in part it states: You can lead us along the pathway to the more abundant life. We blundering grown-ups need in our lives the virtues that you have in yours: The joy and enthusiasm of looking forward to each new day with glorious expectations of wonderful things to come....The vision that sees the world as a splendid place....The radiant curiosity that finds adventure in simple things....The tolerance that forgets differences as quickly as your childish quarrels are spent ~ that holds no grudges, that hates never, that loves people for what they are....the genuineness of being oneself; to be finished with sham, pretense, and empty show; to be simple, natural, and sincere....the courage that rises from defeat and tries again....The believing heart that trusts others, knows no fear and has faith in a divine Father who watches over His children from the sky....the contented trusting mind....we would become like you that we may find again the kingdom of heaven within our hearts.

When you first come in contact with the mentally handicapped person, you may experience strong emotions about the situation. You may feel embarrassment, anger, sadness. These emotions are there because of your strong desire for these people not to be this way. But keep in mind that they have learned to accept it and therefore you too should try to be accepting of it. Not only accepting, but grateful.

Yes, they realize there are things they do not comprehend and things they cannot figure out. Little children are the same way. Children do not sit around worried or angry because they do not understand or think in the deep ways their parents do; they just run off and play and enjoy doing what they can do. Whenever they need an answer to something they cannot figure out, hey ask someone who knows. It does not bother them to ask. Indeed, this spirit of innocent inquiry is what Jesus wants us to have with him. We should realize that we do not have all the answers and be willing to go to God's Word for them. Then, we are to smile, be happy and contented with what we are told, and go on our way.

There is much we can learn from the mentally handicapped in the way of child-like acceptance of things. However, these people cannot share this with us unless we make friends with them. Some people do not know what to say. Say the same things you would to anyone you first meet. Exchange names, ask where they live, ask about their families. Then get a conversation going about the weather, hobbies, an interesting TV program, favorite types of food, favorite types of music, etc.

When you first make friends, you may find that they follow you around after that whenever they see you. Rise to the challenge. Obviously they do not have many friends ~ or perhaps you are their only friend. Take them by the hand and introduce them to other people. Tell the other people about something interesting in that person's life that would make a good topic of conversation. This will help the new people see that a normal type of conversation can be held with them and they can indeed be friends. If sometimes you cannot understand what they are trying to tell you, or they do not understand what you are trying to tell them, just smile and say so. "I don't believe I'm doing a very good job of understanding what you're trying to explain right now. Why don't you try telling me another time and I bet I will then? That's such a pretty color you are wearing today...."

What else can you do for them besides have friendly conversation with them? You could call them on the telephone sometimes. You could send them a note in the mail (letters thrill us all, no matter how young or old). You could stop by and take them with you for a ride to get them out of the house. They miss doing things other people do ~ going to a restaurant, going to a concert or play, going to a ball game, going to a movie, going to the zoo. Take them to some of these places sometimes.

To make sure they act properly for each occasion, do as you would a child. Explain how to act, what to say, whether people are usually quiet or noisy, etc. They will understand, and they will try to be accepted just as much as anyone else. They will try very hard to follow your guidance and example. If a problem arises in public, do as you would a child and quietly re-explain the proper actions. It is not likely that very many people will notice that the person you are with is mentally handicapped. But if they do and seem to be embarrassed for you, just smile broadly at the person you are with, smile broadly at the stranger, and let them know everything is just fine.

Also, try to introduce them to others who are in like circumstances as they. They need a few friends with the same background, just as we all do. They will encourage one another and give advice to one another, and provide a closeness among each other that we cannot. You may wish to take them on outings, such as those mentioned above. Or they may wish to have a picnic together, or birthday parties, or have a hayride, or go bicycling or any number of group activities that young people like to do. Encourage them, and help them find ways to do these things in settings where they are free to be themselves without possible ridicule from people who do not understand them and have not learned to love them yet as you have.

Some people may be afraid they might "get the notion" to get married. This is true. They do feel love as strongly as anyone else. More and more are marrying each other in today's society as we are learning to let them out of the closet and join us. They know their limitations and do not mind asking advice when needed. Having children, they realize, would be difficult for hem to handle, and we need to trust them to work this out acceptably. They need the closeness of family, and as their parents get older, they will still have each other.

Have devotional times with them. Again, as little children, they have a special relationship with God that we need to look upon as an example to us. They may not understand the Bible well enough to distinguish a lot of sins; however, as a child they will follow whatever you explain to them the Bible says to do or not do. They will read simple parts of the Bible, and memorize verses. They accept simply and deeply that there is an invisible God who is with them wherever they go, sees them whatever they do, hears their prayers, and loves them. They will readily sing praises to God in their own faltering but enthusiastic way. They will pray to God in innocent and unwavering faith.

They will love you for showing them the Jesus who loves them. They want to live with him in heaven someday. You could even have a Bible class for them in a home and at your church building. This would be a wonderful community outreach, and the grateful parents would want to come themselves to find out more about people who would love their children as they are.

In addition to helping the mentally handicapped, keep on the watch for things they can do to help others. They can do the same things for others that most teenagers can do. They can help clean up a house or yard of an elderly person. They can walk down the street and take a flower to someone who is sick. They can put together a simple recipe and send it to a family with illness. They can sew for the needy. They can make wooden toys. They can repair bicycles for children and furniture for grownups.

Look for special talents they have. You understand how an arm can be amputated and the remaining arm become extremely strong to compensate. The mind of a mentally handicapped person can be the same way. Sometimes they can perform musically and create artistically in a brilliant manner. They may have a fantastic memory for rote facts, often with numbers. hey can remember statistics from the Bible, or people's ages, or years of significant Bible events. They may have memorized entire chapters or books of the Bible. These are marvelous things to share with others. Why not ask them to recite before a Bible class or special group? This could be a "good work" for them to do for others as a form of teaching about God and his marvels.

Their desire to help others is unsurpassable. They want to be servants of their heavenly Father, and help make God's children happy. Their loyalty to a task will be undying. Oh what examples they can be to us!

And so, my dear friends, you see that you can make the handicapped the center of your good works. There are many types of handicaps. You probably find within yourself at this point in your life the capacity and ability to help one of these types better than any of the others. And so that is who you should help. You could not possibly get around to all of them and do justice, so concentrate on what you feel you have a gift for. Encourage your friends to reach out to those that they feel they can communicate with the best. Each of you has your own ability. Use it. Reach out with it. Clasp a special life with special life-time needs, and soar to God with them!

5 ~ NEWCOMERS

Have you ever moved to a completely new community where you did not know anyone? Chances are in this modern mobile society of ours, you have. Try to remember your thoughts as you arrived, and your many questions.

"Will the people here be friendly and accept us?" "Where is the best place to go grocery shopping?" "Is there a Sears store nearby?" "Will we have to pay a deposit for telephone service here?" "Where will we go to church?" "Will they have a service station that can service our make car?" "Are there any good restaurants?" "Are there any places to go camping nearby?" "How much are hunting and fishing licenses here?" "Do they have a little league team?" "Do they have scouts here?" "What are the schools like?" And on and on we go with our wondering.

The Old Testament scriptures are very explicit regarding treatment of strangers. In fact, there are 228 verses, to be exact, in the Old Testament referring to being a stranger or how to treat a stranger. Exodus 23:9 commands, *Also you shall not oppress a stranger, for you know the heart of a stranger, seeing you were strangers in the land of Egypt* (KJV). This reminder of the Jews having been strangers in Egypt was repeated over and over throughout the hundreds of years that followed. More specifically, Leviticus 19:9,10 tells the Jews to glean their harvest only once and not go back and pick up what was missed. *You shall leave them for the poor and stranger* (KJV). You may recall that Ruth, the widowed Moabitess, was both poor and a stranger when she accompanied her mother-in-law Naomi back to Bethlehem.

Naomi told Ruth to go to a field and walk behind the harvesters, picking up what was left behind (Ruth 2:2). In fact, handsome Boaz happened to be there that first day, noticed her, and asked his servants who that young lady was. Then he ordered his servants to drop a little extra on purpose so she wouldn't have to glean so long to get what she needed. That was the one thing that made her realize Boaz was interested in her personally. So she let him know she was available according to the Jewish custom. Then there was a wedding in Bethlehem. Ruth and Boaz were brought together by a simple kindness to a stranger.

Number 9:14 explains that if a stranger among the Jews wishes to keep the Passover with them, he may do so. A modern way of saying it is, if a stranger wants to go to worship services with you, let him. Of course, you don't know whether he wants to or not unless one of you brings up the subject.

The Jews had cities of refuge for those accused of killing someone where they escaped to until their trial. These cities were to be made available to the Hebrew, the stranger (another nationality), and the sojourner (Numbers 35:12-15). Here, then, is another need fulfilled by the Old Law. Those in trouble could find help. This is, indeed, why some people do move to another community - to escape trouble behind them. The Jews were to help them until there was proof they were guilty.

There was a strong warning to the Jews to judge equally between themselves and the strangers among them (Deuteronomy 1:16). They were not to favor the person they had known for years. It is hard to judge a stranger wisely, but it must be done. Perhaps the best way is to postpone judgment until you get to know him/her better.

The strangers are put in the same category with widows and fatherless in Deuteronomy 10:18. The strangers were to be loved just as much. They were to be treated equally by being given both food and clothing. When people arrive in a new town, they often will have spent most of their money on the move, restaurant meals, and motels. If they haven't obtained housing yet, they will have to continue with these expensive accommodations and meals for a while longer. They need our love and help during this transition time in every way possible.

Even before the Law of Moses was written, strangers were cared for. Job, who lived possibly around the time of Abraham, stated, But no stranger had to spend the night in the street, for my door was always open to the traveler (Job 31:32). Job should be an example to this as well as other methods. He showed God to these strangers by showing them love (1 John 4:8).

Every three years the Jews were to bring the tithe of their fields' increase to the city gates, and there allow the Levites (priestly tribe), the fatherless and the widows, and the strangers to eat and be satisfied (Deuteronomy 14:28,29). They were to do this also yearly at the Feast of Passover, Feast of Weeks, and Feast of Tabernacles (chapter 16). When we have potluck dinners, do we invite the strangers among us? Have we ever had a potluck dinner especially for strangers?

In the New Testament John wrote a letter to Gaius praising him for his treatment of his brethren who were passing through and whom he had taken in:

Dear friend, you are faithful in what you are doing for the brothers, even though they are strangers to you. They have told the church about your love. You will do well to send them on their way in a manner worthy of God. It was for the sake of the Name that they went out, receiving no help from the pagans. We ought therefore to show hospitality to such men so that we may work together for the truth (3 John 5-8).

Yes, just by keeping a preacher in your home while he holds a gospel meeting is helping him and giving you an opportunity to be a fellow worker with him. Whenever a group of Christians comes to your town for a special campaign of knocking on doors, etc., do you keep one or two of them in your home? When you do, you are being a fellow worker with them. So, even though you may not feel you have the same talents they have, can be just as important and necessary to their work. Certain widows are to be supported by the church, lest the church be considered worse than infidels or unbelievers (1 Timothy 5:3-8). However, not just any widow is to be accepted for this.

No widow may be put on the list of widows unless she is over sixty, has been faithful to her husband, and is well known for her good deeds, such as bringing up children, showing hospitality, washing the feet of the saints, helping those in trouble and devoting herself to all kinds of good deeds (1 Timothy 5:9,10).

Notice, one of the requirements is that she have a reputation for good works, including showing hospitality to strangers. Although we should not do these good works for this reason alone, we should remember that one day any of us could be in need, and this will be one of the ways the church will have of judging our worthiness to receive monetary help. (See chapter on benevolence for more on this.) At any rate, helping strangers is considered a very important work, a required work.

God admonished in Hebrews 13:1,2, *Keep on loving each other as brothers. Do not forget to entertain strangers, for by so doing some people have entertained angels without knowing it.* Twice in the Old Testament angels were entertained, and ended up bringing an even greater blessing with them than was given to them by their host.

God appeared to Abraham in the form of a man, with two of his angels. Abraham begged them to stay and eat and rest. He then "hastened" into Sarah's tent to tell her to "make ready quickly" some bread. Then he "ran unto the herd" to get a calf, and "hasted to dress it." After their meal they told Abraham and Sarah that they would have their promised child, even though they were now ages 89 and 99. When the couple doubted, the reply was, "Is anything too hard for the Lord?" (Genesis 18:14).

You may wonder, "How can I ever entertain an angel unaware?" Remember, "Is anything too hard for the Lord?" Who knows but that the stranger you have into your home next time will end up being one of the greatest blessings of your life? You will always receive a blessing from doing this, but sometimes you will even receive an added blessing you never dreamed of. Try it. Then you will understand.

Another example of what welcomed angels did is to give advice and warning to avoid pending trouble. These same angels warned Abraham that Sodom and Gomorrah were going to be destroyed because of their awful sins. They later went to Lot's house to tell him the same thing. In fact, they spent the night there trying to get him and his family to leave. Lot and his wife and daughters believed the warning, but his sons-in-law would not pay any attention.

The next morning, they were still lingering, possibly in hope that the sons-in-law and other family members would change their minds. Finally, the angels literally took them by the hand and rushed them out of the city crying, "Escape for your life!" It was just in time, for the fire fell on the two cities even before they reached their hiding place (Genesis 18:16-19:26).

It may be that one of those you help in your own home may be able later to help you teach and warn your family or friends who have not yet become Christians so they will not suffer a fiery condemnation. Angels are technically messengers from God. In the book of Revelation chapters 2 and 3, angels are referred to as humans, such as "To the angel of the church in Ephesus write...." (2:1). Unknown blessings always await those who entertain strangers in their home.

One of the most exciting prospects of helping strangers is that every time we take in a stranger, we are doing this to Christ, entertaining Christ unawares, so to speak (Matthew 25:40). What a privilege to be able to help our Lord. We all wish at one time or another that we'd been able to see him in his earthly form and do things for him as did Mary and Martha and Lazarus, as well as others of his friends. Well, we can do the next best thing, except that it is two-in-one: our stranger and Jesus both at the same time. A double blessing!

But how does one find the strangers and newcomers to the community? One way would be to contact your Travelers Aid Society if you live in a large city. They give help to people traveling through on a very limited income, and request that the travelers pay them back once they arrive at their destination. Often times they assist someone whose car has broken down and will take several days to be fixed, if they have only enough money to take them straight to their destination. You may contact this organization and ask how you could help, and indicate your willingness to be called on if needed.

Here again, you must decide whether you can take the person into your home until they are able to go on their way. Remember, be as wise as a serpent and harmless as a dove. It is a shame that our society has gotten to the point we have to consider our personal safety. Hopefully, you will be comfortable helping them in your home; however, if you are not, help them find a motel or room at the YMCA or YWCA that fills their needs, and provide transportation from where their car is being worked on and back again in the mornings. You may be comfortable having them over for meals, and this would be most welcome. You can also fix meals in a paper sack to eat while waiting on their car to be repaired, and also to eat on their way to their destination once repairs are completed.

Do you ever stop and help a traveler on the road whose car has broken down or who has run out of gas? If you are a woman alone, there would be some hesitation to stop; but you could lock your door and roll your window part-way down and ask if there is anyone you can call for them. Have you ever been stalled on a road and counted 10, 25, even 100 cars pass by without caring? Sure it is risky to some degree in our age, but so is the mere act of riding in a car. And how do you think the stranded person feels when they aren't sure it is safe to get out of their car? Use care and caution mingled with kindness (wise as serpents, harmless as doves) and you should be able to help in some way without any problems. Just remember they too may be afraid of you. What is the saying? "A better world begins with me."

People moving into a new town very often do not yet have a place to live. If you meet such people, tell them which newspapers or agencies are the best in locating housing. Ask them which part of town they want to live in; schools, location, churches, recreation are all considerations. Perhaps take them in your car driving around looking since you know the streets better than they, and they can save their energies for getting in and out of the car at various locations being considered. This is very exhausting, and someone else doing the driving and knowing the streets without using a map is a priceless gift of friendship to a stranger to your town.

If these people do not find a place to live the first day (it would be very unusual if they did), make sure they have a place to spend the night(s). If they have funds, recommend a motel that is reasonable; they may prefer one with weekly rates and a kitchenette. In some instances, you may wish to let them stay with you, but be sure this is what you truly want to do so you do not end up in a "Rescue/Persecution Triangle" referred to in a previous chapter. If you do not feel comfortable with this and they do not have funds to stay in a motel, you may approach the church or a Traveler's Aid organization. For single individuals, the YMCA and YWCA are possibilities for temporary rooms.

Another need these strangers to town may have is finding a job. Tell them of various large companies who do a lot of hiring that they may qualify for. Gather up some newspapers for them, and go through them together to explain what types of companies these are running the ads.

Perhaps go with them to apply for their jobs. You may stay out in the car or in the lobby, but your presence that close could be a great morale booster. Job hunting is one of the most exhausting things to the ego and the body there is to go through. Help keep their spirits up. You may also personally know of people in businesses that might be interested in hiring someone like this. You will become very tired helping people in this way; but just remember, they are probably five times more tired than you are.

Then there are the strangers who come to your town to make your community their home and who already have lined up their job and their home. These are the lucky ones. They are ready for the step that may come later in helping those mentioned above. This step is helping them get settled into the community and establish themselves as part of the community. How do you learn about them? It used to be the utility company or telephone company was willing to send you a monthly list of all newcomers established in an apartment or house along with their address, unless an individual requests their name not be included. Chambers of Commerce nearly always receive these lists themselves. Real estate companies have contact with newcomers also. Welcome Wagon may share their lists. Following up with these people could keep you busy full time.

First, after you have received your list, you or one of your Bible classes may wish to make up a packet of informational materials to either mail or take in person to the newcomers. You may wish to send a welcome letter and tell them you will be mailing or stopping by with the packet in a few days. Most people who receive just a letter, regardless of how friendly it is, appreciate it and then forget it.

Whatever you decide about a follow-up, a letter is still a good gesture and a very good door opener. It could read something like this:

We just learned that you have moved to our community, and we wanted to be sure and welcome you. We love people and enjoy so much meeting new friends.

This is a time of excitement for you, no doubt, and also a time of innumerable questions. You may wonder....

1. Where are the best places to shop?
2. What types of entertainment does our town have?

3. *Where are the outdoor recreational spots?*
4. *Where are the churches?*
5. *Where are good hunting and fishing spots and how much for licenses?*
6. *Where do we go for new auto and driver licenses?*
7. *What cultural activities do they have?*
8. *Do they have scouts here?*
9. *What types of employment opportunities do they have?*
10. *Where are the doctors and hospitals?*

We would like to stop by in a few days and bring you materials introducing our town, and explain these things to you. Naturally, we will be happy to answer any other questions you have. Most of all, we wish to make you feel really welcome into our community.

We look forward to meeting you in person in a few days. God bless you.

Very sincerely, _____

You will want to enclose a list of your Bible classes and worship services and starting times.

Now, here is a list of things to include in your packet. You will probably think of other things to include or substitute some items:

1. Map of your town (from Chamber of Commerce)
2. Map of your county
3. Map of your state
4. Brochure on hunting and fishing licenses (from your Fish and Game Department)
5. Recent newspaper
6. Entertainment and recreation information (from Chamber of Commerce, Department of Recreation, etc.)

7. Latest employment bulletin (from State/Provincial Employment Office)

8. Brochure from County Health Department

9. Drivers License booklet

10. Your latest church bulletin

11. Brief tract explaining the church

12. A paper explaining the Christian ministries being done by your congregation

13. A card explaining the times of worship and Bible classes

14. Coupon book of a "welcome wagon" type. Your congregation may even want to create a small one of your own by contacting a few businesses and saying the church will pick up the tab within certain limits.

15. Anything else you can think of.

See if someone will go with you to deliver the packets. You should not try to see very many families in a month, for you should be able to remain in contact with them and make friends with them. If you have too many people to follow up with, you will spread yourself too thin, especially if you eventually set up a home Bible study with them. So perhaps you can get some of your friends to help also.

The husband-wife team is best because it may be that only the wife is home or only the husband is home when you arrive, and it might make the visit awkward. Tell them a little about yourself, and find out about them in a friendly but not-too-curious way. Discover their hobbies and interests. Learn the names of their children if you can. Be friends with them. Remember, they are strangers, and probably know few if any people in your town yet. It is very lonely for them still, no matter how busy they may be moving in.

After you have been there a few minutes chatting, open the packet and hand the items to them one at a time, explaining anything else you want to about each item. Invite them to worship and Bible class when you get to the church materials. Most people do not care especially where they go to worship, and often choose a place merely by how close it is to home, or if they know someone there.

You might offer to help them unpack, although many people prefer to do it themselves so they'll know where everything is. If they need to go to a certain office in town, offer to pick them up and take them over the first time, and show them places of interest on your way.

Before you leave, invite them to your home sometime in the future. If they are still manipulating boxes, invite them over the next day if possible, for it is terribly hard to cook amidst a moving conglomeration. It doesn't have to be a fancy meal. They will appreciate the chance to get away from all that unpacking regardless.

If they put off attending Bible class with you, offer to take their children. Most people want their children to go, even if they don't themselves. Regardless, contact a few people in your congregation and tell them a little about your newcomer friends ahead of time. This way they can watch for them when they do attend and be sure to greet them with something like, "My friend has told me some very nice things about you, and I have been looking forward to meeting you." Hopefully your friends will invite the new family to their home sometime soon, and thus enlarge their new circle of friends.

By the way, when you invite someone over to your home, never say, "Why don't you come over some time?". That really says nothing very concrete and sincere. If you really mean it, then say, "Why don't you come over next Friday evening?" If they say they are busy that night, then ask if Sunday would be better, or whatever day you wish. But be specific.

Another type of newcomer into our community we do not usually think of is the person in the half-way house. Half-way houses have been set up for people who have been in some type of full-care situation, and are being eased back into society and on their own again. These people are from prisons, drug and alcohol facilities, institutions for the mentally handicapped, physical rehabilitation clinics, mental hospitals, homes for unwed mothers, and some older juvenile facilities.

These people would require more attention and concentration; but at the same time, they have the moral support and guidance of counselors in addition to you. You could probably do with them everything that has been mentioned above for newcomers. Then there are other things you could do.

You could stop by and pick one of these people up and take them for rides to get better acquainted with the community. You could take them around looking at apartments; and if applicable, looking at cars to buy. You could take them around job hunting. If/when they succeed in finding a job but will not be able to buy a car, you could take them through the bus route to get them used to that.

Again, it is necessary with these people at half-way houses to be very careful not to enter the "Rescue Triangle" discussed in the chapter on benevolence. These people are in these half-way houses because of past inability to take care of their own needs, and these people have been having people make more decisions for them than people out living on their own.

They will try to continue this old pattern with you, trying to put decisions on you and actions on you that they could and should be doing alone. Concentrate with them on building up their self-confidence, and in building new social skills. Such skills would be how to interview for a job, how to get along at the office or shop with peers and employers, making appointments on time, working at a task until it is completed, budgeting, etc.

You could encourage them to make contact with their family, whether they are in the same town or another. If they have not been close to their family, try to encourage communication more often and seeing each other. Help them make new friends in the community, and learn how to be selective so that the friends build them up rather than tear them down. Of course encourage them to attend church and make new friends among Christians. There is another category of newcomers to the community who are in some respects perpetual newcomers, for they are only temporary. These are the service personnel and college students. The next chapter will be devoted entirely to what you can do for them, and what you can encourage them to do in turn for others.

A figurative type of newcomer to the community is the newly widowed or divorced. Although living where they may have lived for many years or even all their lives, they usually leave the world of couples and enter the world of singles. Even if they attend functions for couples, they are single regardless. In order to avoid awkwardness which could innocently lead to jealousies, these single adults quite often begin to associate with one another for a social life. However, if they have been part of a couple for many, many years, they may not be close to any single people. Although in the same city, they must enter a new society of people in that city. They usually enter as strangers or relative strangers.

If you know a newly single person, and are acquainted with another single person with similar interests (no match-making please), introduce them. This will be a good beginning. However, do not let go of the person to find their way into the single world on their own from then on. Often newly single-again people will ask, "Where are all my old friends? We've always done things together. Now they hardly talk to me. Do I have leprosy or something? Why don't they call me anymore?" Continue your friendship with them. They needn't be in the single world exclusively. They could be part of both worlds.

Remember, finally, that in a sense we are all strangers, living in a strange country, pilgrims, travelers, on our way to our real home. The author of Hebrews speaks of Christianity in this sense: *Instead, they are longing for a better country ~ a heavenly one. Therefore, God is not ashamed to be called their God; for he has prepared a city for them* (Hebrews 11:16). So let us all help one another as we travel through this life until we arrive at our permanent heavenly home in the world to come.

6 ~ MILITARY PERSONNEL & UNIVERSITY STUDENTS

Many military personnel and most university and college students are away from home for a long period of time for the first time in their lives. Most are teenagers, some as young as 17 up through about age 25.

All service personnel and students are faced with daily temptations far beyond the understanding of most of us not in their generation. At first it may be a little shocking to them, for although teenagers do come across much temptation during high school days, they do not realize it will be so often and with such intensity among young people away from home.

Many of these young people are still going through the growing-up stage of seeing for themselves if Mom and Dad were right. They may take the exact opposite point of view and either discuss it or actually go out and do it, thinking that they might have been told wrong. They are wanting to make the decision for themselves on what is right or wrong as a part of entering their adulthood. If they were taught gambling was wrong and are not totally convinced themselves, when on their own they may begin a little betting just to see first hand. This is not done in a spirit of maliciousness but of experimenting with life to see what really is true.

Some young people are convinced of a moral just by someone they respect explaining it. Others want to see examples of people on both sides. Still others have to try both ways themselves to see. This is a difficult time in a young person's life, as well as those who love them and don't want to see them hurt. They are in need of supportive adults during this time - supportive in helping them stand for good rather than experimenting with the bad.

Influences of people around them is extremely important during this time in their young adulthood. They feel an intense desire to be accepted by their peers. Most of them are basically good young people. However, it only takes one person daring the others to get a whole group doing things they would not ordinarily do alone.

So the challenges continue day after day in the realms of language, dress, sex, drinking, drugs, honesty, etc. God warned of this very thing. He said through Paul in 1 Corinthians 5:8 & 6: *Let us therefore celebrate the feast, not with old leaven, nor with the leaven of malice and wickedness, but with the unleavened bread of sincerity and truth. Your boasting is not good. Do you not know that a little leaven leavens the whole lump?* Paul was writing this because there was a man committing a sin within the congregation and Paul was afraid he would influence the others to follow his example.

Young people need encouragement in speaking out against what is wrong and in favor of what is good. One way is to get them involved in good groups to develop their sense of being good examples. The Bible has several accounts of young people being examples for good. Consider Shadrach, Meshach, Abednego and Daniel in the first few chapters of Daniel in the Old Testament. Consider Joseph as a young person in the house of Potiphar and in the Egyptian prison as related in Genesis 38-41.

These young service personnel and university students have varying degrees of ambition and desire to better themselves; but they all have it in some form. They are not generally associated with that part of young people's society that sits and wants to be handed life's good things. They are willing to work for something. They are intelligent and will for the most part become positive contributors to society. They can be taught to be positive contributors to the Lord's work also.

If you live in a town that has a military base or college or university nearby, you have a great challenge involving much work ~ all extremely rewarding if you can do it. Primarily what needs done is finding the Christians on base or campus, getting them to come to worship services the first time, and then keeping them interested.

These military personnel learning to defend their country in various ways need to be and can be taught to defend the greatest kingdom in the world, the kingdom of God, and with the sword of the Spirit which is the Word of God. These university students developing their minds through libraries full of books need to be taught to develop their spirits through the library of the 66 books in the Bible.

It used to be that finding Christians on the bases and campuses was not hard. On a military base, you could go to the chaplain's office for names by religious affiliation. On a college or university campus, you could get this from the registrar's office. If neither is possible, you may have to try doing a religious survey of your own. If that cannot be done, then ads on bulletin boards and base or campus newspapers should be placed. Any way you can, get names and addresses.

Next, write them a letter. In it you may wish to say merely where the church building is, and invite them to come. You may include a little tract in it that would be appropriate for them. If you do not know of any tracts for military or university people who are Christians, perhaps someone in your congregation would be willing to write one and have it printed.

Your first letter to them will bring out a very small percentage of the people you mailed it to, possibly five percent. However, this will be your nucleus for further growth. These are the self-starters and will probably be the strongest Christians you contact. When they come to services, plan to have them over to your home for a meal. Or if there are more than you can handle, perhaps some other families would like to have part of them in their homes. Being able to go to a home and not have to go back to the barracks or dormitory will be a welcomed change. Don't worry about entertaining them. They will entertain themselves.

Never let your service or university people go back to the base or campus on Sunday afternoon to eat "chow" alone or be too late to eat at all. Offer transportation from the building after that first visit if any had to take the bus, a taxi, or hitchhike. Be available to pick them up for church meetings from then on if they need it.

Ask one or two if you can handle them to spend the weekend with you in your home ~ to sleep in a real bedroom, have home-cooked meals, and real live children to delight them. Whenever your family goes on a picnic, boating trip, etc., invite some of these lonely ones to go with you. You will be richly blessed for it. And try to look them up on the base or campus occasionally if possible.

Leave openings for them to confide in you or your husband. Remember, life in the military or on campus presents more temptations and problems than you may imagine unless you were once there yourself. Don't criticize them for falling into temptation; do encourage them to keep trying to do right.

Just because the student or military person will only be with your community and congregation for a year or two, do not omit them from doing Christian works with you. Some military people are only at a base for a few months. Don't let this deter you, for months grow into years, and then where has their Christianity gone?

Some time soon after their first visit to your home, sit down with them, and go over with them the list of Christians you found on the base or campus. Divide them up among everyone, so that everyone on your list is visited that week and personally invited to services. It shouldn't take long to go through a dormitory or barracks of the ones on their list.

You may double or triple the number of service personnel or students you have the next Sunday. Therefore, plan ahead of time to have a potluck dinner for them if possible, which means each participating family would bring twice as much as they would eat themselves. Have it inside if is a cold or a rainy day; but don't miss the opportunity to have it outside if at all possible. There is something warm and friendly about eating under God's blue cathedral ceiling, with beams from the very trees themselves, and a chandelier made of the sparkling, glittering sun.

After the meal, you may wish to sit in a circle and talk about what it is like being a Christian in the military or on campus. It will be good for the students to see that they are not alone in their temptations, and in their trying to live the way God would be proud of them. They may wish to give each other suggestions on how to handle certain problems that arise in certain groups or classes. Be sure to show them examples from the Bible who had similar problems and how they handled or failed to handle them. Indeed, the Bible contains at least one example of every kind of problem known to man, then and now.

Some Bible examples of young people with problems to face are Noah's sons, Joseph, David, Solomon, Josiah, Vashti, Esther, Daniel, Shadrach, Meshach, Abednego, Peter, Mary Magdalene, Timothy, Titus.

Friday and Saturday nights are the hardest of the week if a single person has nowhere to go out. Set one of these nights aside every week for these young people to all get together for a meal, followed by some sort of entertainment.

A possible Saturday night event may be an open house in your home. You could request that anyone who comes bring a snack to share. Just make your home available for people to pop in and out starting around 7:00 until whenever. You would not be entertaining them; they'd be strictly on their own ~ bring games, watch a video, play the piano, play pool or whatever.

These young people may have some ideas on how to interest those who have not yet started attending worship services and Bible classes. They will doubtless think primarily of forms of entertainment to attract them. But you could also guide them in thinking of some forms of Christian service that may attract them. Remember, one of the reasons people do not come to services is because it has always been "such a bore." What are some forms of Christian service you might help them consider?

They could practice singing hymns together, then go to a nursing home or senior residence to sing. Young ladies can do this alone, or there may be a mixed group. While at the home, they could check to see if they could do this on a regular basis, every Sunday if possible. (For further details, see the chapters on nursing homes and senior housing.) Naturally, after they are through singing, they should make sure everyone in the home is visited for at least five minutes each. It may be that the group or part of the group will want to take them home as a full-time project.

The group may wish to go to the private homes of some homebound individuals and hold a worship service with them every Sunday afternoon. If you are blessed with a large group, they could divide up and go to one or two homes each.

When was the last time anyone did a religious survey in your town to find wayward Christians or people with no religious affiliation? Or how about choosing a large apartment complex and leaving a tract or flier and personally inviting people to attend service? Young people are full of insatiable energy. They could begin on a Saturday morning, come to the building for lunch, and go back out a few hours that afternoon.

Perhaps once a month on a different Friday night, the young people could have a dinner party for the older members of your congregation and their friends, and/or any senior citizens you know of in the community. They may wish to invite an entire senior citizens club. It is often lonely on Friday nights ~ or any other night ~ for them too. This would be a good time to teach the young ladies to cook for crowds. The young men could arrange the tables and pick up guests at home.

If there is a special school or class in your town for mentally handicapped children, your young people may wish to send out invitations for them to come to a little party once a month, perhaps one of the Friday nights. The young people could make favors for them. After refreshments, perhaps someone good at storytelling could tell them a little bit about God and how much he loves them. The regular teacher of those children could give you further ideas on how to work with that particular group of youngsters. You could win the hearts of these parents forever if you took such an interest in the mentally handicapped child, so often neglected by society ~ and possibly win the souls of the parents also.

The young people may wish to go around to each of the businesses in your community to ask if it would be all right to place a tract rack in their business. More than you may think would be willing to do this. Once you have a number of businesses, they can build the racks to be either hung on a wall or set on a counter. Then don't forget to go back and replenish them every week or two.

Are there any widows, single-again women, or service wives whose husbands are gone and need work done on or around their houses? Those permanently with no husband especially could use some help with this. Perhaps these young adults could take one whole Saturday afternoon spring cleaning or winterizing.

Paint the house and fence with donated paint, wash the windows, trim the lawn around the sidewalks, clean out the gutters, clean the garbage pails, clean the carpets, wash the curtains, move the furniture around if desired, clean out the cupboards (only if they want it done), clean their oven, repair the leaks in the roof, put up or take down storm windows. Doing this for a birthday would be a wonderful love gift.

Periodic checks of the automobile are much needed and appreciated also.

Be prepared to think of some way a widow can "repay" or thank you, for she will likely want to do something, even if it is small. Do not deprive her of the opportunity of doing something for you in turn. If she likes to bake ~ and many older women do ~ hint how much you love home-made cookies. Or whatever she can do well, drop a hint or two how good she must be at
doing that. Even better, if she would be willing, she could "repay" you by baking the cookies for someone who is shut in, and passing on the love gifts.

Of course, she may not be able to do anything for anyone else but express her desire to do just something, anything. In that case, when she brings it up, ask her to say a special prayer for all of you every day. This is about as special a gift as she could ever give you!

Do not overlook the older widowers. There don't seem to be as many, but they often need as much help with their houses.

Is the church building near a shopping center? Ask your elders if the young people can put up signs all over the center that free child care is available from 12:30 to 3:30 every Saturday afternoon. Under this, mention that no food will be served. You could set up a regular schedule, much like a Vacation Bible School. Here is a suggested agenda:

12:30 Sing Bible songs and act them out
1:00 Tell or read a Bible story, or show a Bible video and follow with questions to see how much they learned
1:30 Color a picture about the lesson
2:00 Have the children put on headdresses like Bible people and act out the story
2:30 Make a little favor reminding them of the story, like a fish, or star, or treasure, or crown
3:00 Sing songs again and talk about their families
3:30 Time to go home

Tell parents ahead of time that only those who pick up heir children on time may bring them back the following week. You'll have to have this rule to avoid being taken advantage of by a few.

But oh the marvelous opportunities to teach the Bible you could have with such a group of children. Several of them may influence their parents and older brothers/sisters to attend Bible study and worship in that same building on Sundays.

Is there a section of your town that is full of underprivileged children? If so, make a special effort with them. If there is a park near them, knock on doors and pass out printed invitations to join you at the park on Saturday afternoon at 1:00 for a kind of day camp. (You may have to get permission from the Park Commission.)

Have organized play. If a few show up, keep the group together. However, if many show up, divide up into age groups. Play lawn games such as kickball, keep away, cat and mouse, farmer in the dell, Simple Simon among the younger ones. Have a baseball game or volleyball with the older ones. Perhaps the Parks and Recreation Department would be willing to lend you equipment if you need any.

After the games, sit on the ground with the group and ask them if they have heard the Bible story about _____. Then proceed, with their help as much as possible, to tell the story to them. You could possibly assign a praise phrase, or an animal sound or something for them to say in unison whenever the story calls for it.

Do not make the story very long, for their attention span sitting still outdoors is short. Have a small New Testament to read a scripture or two about the story, perhaps for them to memorize.

End with a couple songs about the Bible. Then ask them how many would like to go to Sunday school the next day (on the bus if you have one). Probably they will all raise their hands. Write down their names, addresses and phone numbers. Then tell them you will call them in the morning to see for sure if they can come and can be ready.

No doubt these youngsters will really mean it when they raise their hands and tell you they want to go, and be very enthusiastic at the time. But after you leave, the enthusiasm will wear off. So Sunday morning they may either forget, or their parents will forget or object. Call them at least one hour before time to pick them up to ask them if they still want to go.

Then you or the bus go by a good hour before Bible study starts, for there may even be some you will have to wait for or even go in and help get dressed quickly the first couple times. Tell the parents when you expect to be back. If you use a bus instead of cars, have someone available to lead songs and have bible drills to keep earlier passengers occupied in a productive and controlled manner.

Escort them to their classes when they arrive, and try to keep them quiet and from running. Leave your own class early if you did not stay with them, to be there when they dismiss. Next show them the restrooms and drinking fountains. Then go with them to the auditorium for worship. Explain the order of the service and what kinds of things they will be expected to do - sing, pray with their eyes closed, be quiet, listen. After services, introduce them to some of the grownups, and then escort them to the car or bus.

If the families of these youngsters have not previously attended worship services anywhere for a matter of years, the likelihood of their doing so now is slim. However, do not overlook them. Every now and then invite them. If they do not have a Bible, buy them one if possible. If the parents never do attend, at least you planted the seed. Do stick with the children; make Christianity ingrained in them, so that when they're grown, they will not depart from it.

These are just a few of the things you could guide the university students and young service personnel to do for their Lord as a group. Help them see that Christianity is not being served, but serving others. You can make your home and your talents available to them. Above all, make Christianity a living thing to these young people; for if it is not living, it is dead. There are no other alternatives. And the parents of these young people in the military or at university will bless you for what you have done to encourage their young people away from home!

7 ~ BIBLE SCHOOL CLASSES

When we teach a class, do our students go out and apply in their personal lives what we have taught them? Remember, teaching does not occur until learning has occurred. If we teach them we ought to be good to our neighbors and they do not go out and do good things for their neighbors, they have not learned your lesson. Feeding someone does not occur unless someone eats. We may poke food into someone's mouth, but unless they swallow it, they are not being fed.

In most Bible classes, it goes something like this: Begin with a brief discussion about the main point of the lesson, then read the lesson from the Bible or   storybook, then discuss what it means, and finally close with a brief discussion of how to apply these things to our lives. End with a prayer asking God to help all to be better Christians. Then everyone goes home.

Our Lord did not say we should sit around together and just repeat the things he said. He said we are to learn them and DO the things he said. Otherwise, our calling him Lord or Master is untrue. In some respects, Jesus is our employer and we are working for him. What are we producing for him? There are many possibilities, and they can be easily taught in the classroom.

There are two ways you could adjust your classroom teaching to make sure the students have applied what they learned. You may go ahead and teach like you have been, and then that Wednesday evening when the class assembles again, spend that whole period with a project that is appropriate to the lesson of the prior Sunday. Or all in the same class period you could spend fifteen or twenty minutes reading the lesson and discussing it to make sure the students understand and remember it; then spend the remaining twenty or thirty minutes with a class project applying the lesson.

Doing things together as a class is important, for there is strength in numbers. You may tell your students to do a certain good work during the week, but being alone s/he is not likely to do it, regardless of good intentions. Just as learning facts with other people is more encouraging and more fun, so learning actions with other people is too. Jesus always recommended that his disciples go out at least in twos. Then an individual is more likely, once having learned to do something with others, to do it when alone also. This is genuine teaching.

In Appendix A of this book is an extensive list of good works your students could do in application of most of the events in the Bible commonly taught in children's classes. You will probably think of other works in some instances, and whatever best fits your situation is what you should do. You may wish to have a different good work each week or one that covers an entire month. You will notice that intermingled with the giving of time and talents is the giving of money. All three are part of giving and part of works, and children love to do all three.

Perhaps the day your children are to give money for a good cause, if they are very young, you could bring soft drink bottles/cans to give them and let them "cash them in" at a pretend store with a toy cash register in the corner of your room. There are other ways you could show very young children how they could earn money for the Lord when they are a little older

For older children, a week before they are to bring money for a good work, you could put up a sign on the bulletin board asking that anyone wanting some odd jobs done, such as raking leaves, could sign up. If the parents are willing to take the child to that house sometime during the week, that would give them an opportunity to visit with Christian friends while waiting for their child to do the work. The people having the work done just pay whatever they wish. However, it is worked out, the children earn their own money and from this make a free-will offering. Discourage several of them going together in a project such as washing cars or a bake sale. This would create the impression the church is becoming a business. The only examples we have in the Bible is of individuals raising their own money, whether it be by contributing jewelryy or selling land or going out and earning it. 1 Corinthians 16:2 explains, On the first day of every week, EACH ONE OF YOU should set aside a sum of money in keeping with his income. Giving is an individual responsibility. This will teach much to the children.

Many of the projects suggested in the appendix are writing and drawing projects so the children may send messages of concern and love to various people. Generally the supplies you will need are: [1] colored paper, [2] crayons, [3] glue, [4] glitter, [5] paper doilies, etc. for decorations, [6] notebook paper, [7] pencils, [8] envelopes, [9] stamps, [10] telephone book, [11] decorated box to collect food in, [12] box to collect clothing in, [13] Bible bank to collect Bible money in, [14] magazines for pictures, [15] work smocks or shirts, [16] tape recorder and tapes, [17] copy of a magazine listing missionaries, [18] camera.

The camera is an added item that is not necessary but nice to have. Take pictures of your class working on their good works. Put the photos on your bulletin board. Sometimes put them on the bulletin board used by the whole congregation. Make a scrapbook.

Occasionally you may wish to write a news story and send it and a photo or two to your local newspaper. Christian magazines may be interested in a story and picture. You will encourage non-Christians in your community to want to be part of your class, as well as encourage other Christians to add such Christian works to their own classes and lives.

One caution if you do send in newspaper articles. Do not boast about what you and your class are doing. Christian works are not anything extra ~ they are a requirement to being Christian. By the grace of God, you have enough materials possessions that you can help others in these ways.

You are doing these things to bring a blessing on others and glory to your Savior, not to yourselves. If you receive the praise of people for doing these things, you already have your reward. It is those who do things without boasting, but in humility, who receive their reward later on from God (Matthew 6:5,6). You cannot be rewarded by both. Just think of it this way: It is not I, but Christ who lives in me (Galatians 2:20) who is doing these things.

Those of you teaching older students may wish to make out a confidential questionnaire to give them. Without it you may teach them for two or three years and never realize some things about them that would be helpful to both you and the class as a whole. Here is a suggestion of what you could ask:

1. Name
2. Address

3. School

4. Favorite Subject

5. Hobbies and/or Pastimes

6. Favorite Reading Material

7. Club/Team Memberships

8. Your Ideal Person

9. Why?

10. Favorite Type Music

11. Occupational Ambition

12. Life's Goal

13. Plans for Next Summer

14. Talents (even if you're the only one who thinks so)

15. Pet Peeves

16. Are you a Christian?

   If yes, when, where, by whom baptized

   If no, why?

17. What can you do for Jesus?

18. What would you like to learn to do for Jesus?

19. What subjects would you like to study in this class?

20. Are you willing to do homework for this class?

21. Please list your friends from Christian families who do not attend.

22. Please list your friends from non-Christian families who you would like the class to visit.

   ___ In a group?

   ___ On Sunday afternoon

   ___ On weekend evening

You may think of other questions to add or as substitutes, depending on your group. At any rate, it would give you an idea of where your class is spiritually and background wise. For instance, if no one is interested in visiting, they need extra teaching on this. In the meantime, they can do works that are not so personal. Also you can work out some class projects for them based on their talents and interests, some projects you may not even have thought of otherwise. Probably with older students, this should be a unanimous selection of the class.

Here is another way to develop responsibility in your older students. Arrange a confidential chart that no one will ever see but them. Use a half piece of paper inside a piece of colored paper folded with their name on the front. This half sheet will hold six months. List months and

Sundays along the top. Along the side in a double-spaced column list the following titles only. Below that, relist the titles but also include percent values of each.

        10%   On-time
        10%   Brought Bible
        10%   Brought Assignment
        10%   Brought Notebook
        15%   Brought Guest
        15%   Contacted an absentee
        15%   Read Bible Daily
        15%   Prayed for Non-Christian
        100% TOTAL POSSIBLE

For those still catching on to the idea of the Christian life of works such as these youngsters, often something tangible such as this chart is helpful so they can see how they are progressing.

Have a supply of "We Missed You" postcards on hand for all the students to sign and send to anyone who missed class. Keep a record of what cards you sent to whom, so you do not duplicate any. Religious supply stores have this type of card in abundance.

Midweek classes are to just fill our time. Right? NO! NO! A thousand times NO! Midweek classes can provide the greatest opportunities of any time of the week, even above Sunday. This is the time when you can interest the most students in coming to your class who attend somewhere else on Sundays, or whose family goes somewhere on the weekends, etc. Especially during the long summer days is this a popular time, for kids want somewhere to go that is not too late in the evening.

Make your midweek class especially interesting to outsiders. Make it an evening Vacation Bible School that never ends. Make it a WEDNESDAY-CATION BIBLE SCHOOL. Make this a special evening for them, an evening they will not want to go home from because of all the fun they've had learning God's word and will for their lives. Have rewards for those who bring friends just as summer Vacation Bible School does. Have rousing songs. Duplicate as much as possible what you do during VBS, and see Wednesday nights take on a new gusto. Give them real learning experiences and your class and the entire congregation ultimately will grow beyond your fondest expectations.

When you have visitors to your class, regardless of the age of your students, do follow up with them. Welcome buttons or tags are nice to give them. Then you could send a postcard or letter telling them how glad you were to have them in class. You could stop by to see them a few minutes or phone them during the week and get acquainted with the rest of the family. It would certainly reassure the family that they have available to them such nice teachers as you who are interested in them personally. Visiting is almost a lost custom today, at least in the post-industrial countries. If possible, show them it is not lost in Christianity.

Another nice custom to have in your class is a birthday remembrance. Have birthday buttons on hand with a Bible verse written on them if possible. Pass a card around the classroom for the students to all sign, and give it to the one with the birthday, or mail it the day before their birthday. After all, we are indeed glad they were born, and glad God brought them our way to bless our lives a little more.

Get your class together once a month or at least once quarterly, and go around in a carload, stopping by briefly at the home of anyone who has been absent for a long time to let them know they are missed. Tell them you are all going to stop and get a coke after you visit two or three others and ask if they'd like to squeeze in the car and join you. Be sure you don't dress up too much for this outing so they will feel at ease to "come as you are." Also if there is a friend of one of your students who is interested in starting to class, stop by and see them a minute too and invite them to go along.

At the end of each quarter you could have a Bible-times party and let the kids dress up like their favorite character from the stories you have discussed in class. You could play twenty questions to guess who they are. This would be a marvelous way to review. Then have them sit on the floor and eat the foods Bible-times people ate. You could have a party with each one dressed up like one type person we can help, such as someone in the hospital, a baby, someone elderly, someone in jail, someone with lots of children, etc. Or, if your class has been studying Paul's missionary journeys, or learning about missionaries all over the world today, each one could pretend s/he is one of those missionaries and be called by that missionary's name. Or they could dress like the people of a particular country; then your games could center around those countries.

At the end of each party, after all games and refreshments, always have a brief devotional. This will teach your students that no matter what they are doing or where they are, God is there and should be thanked for all things, even fun. You are nearly to the end of this chapter. It was a short one only because so much of it is continued in Appendix A in the back of this book. Technically, you will not be done with the chapter until you have looked it over. So, as soon as you come to the end of this page, look immediately at Appendix A for the real conclusion.

Jesus was a great teacher, a master teacher, and him we must follow. Regardless of his message, he still attracted people because he went about practicing what he taught and showing others how to practice it. The other teachers of his day were much like many of today's teachers ~ standing before a group, telling some things, and then sending everyone on their way. They were not good leaders and were jealous of Jesus.

Jesus lived what he taught and showed his followers step by step how to live what he taught them. Coupled with the greatest message on earth, he became the greatest teacher in the history of the world. Follow his examples and aspire to be like him.

~~~~~~~~~~~~~~~~~~~~~~

See also my book, *The Old Old Story Set to Old Old Tunes,* 40 songs on the Old Testament and 40 songs on the New Testament, all set to old American folk tunes.

See also my book, *Fun With Bible Numbers,* 500 arithmetic problems on the entire Bible.

8 ~ CRAFTSMANSHIP

Chef. Tailor. Artisan. Craftsman. Perhaps you prefer to do things with your hands more than your intellect. You'd rather make something than read something. Or you get home from work and you need something to do to unwind that's not mental. Perhaps you're retired and don't take life so seriously anymore. You have abilities to do your Christian works right there at home.

Some Bible men used their building and carving and designing skills for others. Bezaleel and Aholiab were famous for using their skills on furniture, engravings, and tapestries for the tabernacle (Exodus 35:30-35).

Some Bible women used their homemaking talents and abilities to help others. The widow at Zarephath baked for Elijah and gave him a room to stay in during a drought (1 Kings 17:7-24). The Shunamite woman provided a room for the prophet Elisha to stay in whenever he was in the area (2 Kings 4:8-37). Peter's mother-in-law fed Jesus and his companions (Luke 4:38,39). Whenever Jesus was in Bethany, he went to the home of Martha and Mary (Luke 10:38-42). Dorcas sewed clothing for the poor (Acts 9:36-41). The elect or chosen lady to whom John wrote his second published letter was thanked for taking in traveling gospel teachers.

Now, how can these talents be used today for Christian service? First, let's talk about what women like to do.

Dorcas, the account in Acts 9 says, was full of good works and helping the poor. When she died, she was laid out in an upper chamber. Her friends learned that the apostle Peter was in a nearby town, so sent for him to come quickly. Were they wanting him to come in time for the funeral, or were they hoping he could perform a miracle? We do not know.

But Peter must have thought a great deal of Dorcas, for he rushed to where she was as quickly as he could. When he arrived, there were many widows there in that upper chamber weeping for her. They showed Peter the coats and dresses Dorcas had made for them.

There must have been something very special about Dorcas. For Peter asked for a few moments alone with her. Then he knelt down, prayed fervently for her soul to return, and it did. He told Dorcas to rise up, she opened her eyes, sat up, and Peter gave her his hand for her to stand up. Then he opened the door where her friends were waiting, and presented her alive to them! The one chosen to be brought back from death was a woman who made clothing for the poor!

Those of you who sew have much you can do. So first, let us investigate where some good places are to get your yard goods. If you live near a fabric mill, you may ask them for their rejected yardage and tell them it is for church work. (They can deduct this donation from their taxes.)

You could also make it known in your congregation that you need fabric scraps. Perhaps you could place a box at an appropriate place for people to put their scraps if they don't see you personally. Some fairly new articles of clothing are sometimes torn beyond repair, but the material is still good. Or perhaps your Christian friends have articles of clothing that are out of style, such as suits and ties, that could be cut up and remade into something else. And of course you know that many children's clothes can be made from scraps leftover from making larger items, and also from larger clothes cut down. These clothes could be put in the church's "clothes closet," they could be sent to children's homes, state hospitals, nursing homes, shelters for the homeless, or sent overseas for a missionary to distribute among the poor there. Remember those missionaries who live where there are few if any clothing stores from which to purchase their own clothing.

Quilts are another need among the underprivileged, both in our own nation and in nations overseas. It takes more time to make one quilt, but smaller scraps leftover from making clothing can be recycled and put to use. Quilts can be made on a sewing machine; they don't have to be a work of art when numbers is more important. Any way you look at it, however, quilts will take more time to make than clothing. But just remember that, whereas the clothing will only last awhile. The quilts will undoubtedly serve their good purpose for many years.

You can recycle old nylons and use them for stuffing little play animals. These quiet little toys can be used in the church nursery for crying babies. They can be kept on hand for gifts for children whom you help with clothing. They could be given to the teacher of very young tots to use as gifts.

Quiet books can be made to give little children to look at during worship services. Make the pages out of white muslin or oilcloth. On one page you could sew a pocket. On another page you could sew a piece of material shaped like a dress with a real zipper all the way up. On the next page you could sew a piece of material shaped like a shirt and put real buttons and buttonholes on it. Next you could get some fuzzy material and make a glove for the child to put its hand in. Then you could have a little Raggedy-Ann-type face with yarn hair to braid and button nose and eyes. On another page you could have a pretend shoe with a real shoelace in it so the child can learn to tie. Use your imagination, and you probably can come up with some other ideas that will intrigue little ones and make them nice and quiet.

You can make lap robes and shawls for older people in nursing homes and hospitals. If you can knit, you can make sweaters for babies, children, and adults. You can make little booties to be taken by the nursery teacher as gifts from the church to new parents in the community; this would show them we love their little babies and would like to teach them how much God loves them too.

Make costumes for the children's Bible classes so they can act out their Bible stories with a little more realism. Bible-times robes are not hard to make. Sandals could be made of cardboard and shoelaces or yarn.

If you can crochet or embroider, you can make bookmarks for Bibles to be used as gifts to newcomers, visitors, newlyweds, people with new babies, birthdays, perfect attendance, Vacation Bible School awards, etc. Bookmarks are small and do not take long to make, but can be used and appreciated by everyone.

Make curtains for classrooms. Curtains could be kept on hand to help people "starting over" after a fire, tornado, etc. or financial setback.

In the midst of all your house caring, don't forget to be on the lookout for anyone who does not know how to use skills you have and would like to learn. There are things they possibly want to do for their family in this area. Or they may be looking for ways to help others from their homes. Take time to invite them to your home and teach them to be a worker too.

Perhaps cooking is the thing you love to do. Teach with cookies. The nursery teachers always have a snack during their class time with the little ones. Find out what they will be talking about each week, and help teach them with your cookies. If the lesson is about Adam and Eve, make your cookies in the shape of a tree. If it is about an animal such as a sheep, try to locate a cookie cutter in that shape. If the lesson has something to do with the temple or tabernacle, make your cookies in the shape of an altar. If it is about Jonah or the fishing apostles or the miracle of fishes, make your cookies look like fish. If it is about the death of Jesus, make them in the shape of a cross. If it is about Paul's missionary journey, make them look like boats. The ideas for lessons are endless and very meaningful.

During Vacation Bible School time, there is a need for many dozens of cookies every day. You could make and freeze them during the winter and spring months in preparation for this. And keep in mind youth activities such as Bible Bowls, youth rallies, encampments, "half-time" football parties.

When there is a birthday in a nursing home or children's home, or among those in your congregation without a family nearby such as widow, widower, college student or service person, you could bake a birthday cake for them. Keep on hand a sugar-free cake recipe for older people prone to diabetes.

Whenever you learn of someone who is ill, bake a casserole for them. In some instances, a roast chicken is very economical and nutritious; but of course there are numerous other good dishes. Try to include fresh vegetables and/or fruit. If there is a dessert included, try to make it nutritious. People under strain always need extra nutrition to help keep them from becoming too run down physically and mentally. This also applies when there is a death in someone's family, and they do not feel like cooking; or you can take your food to the funeral dinner. Be sure to put your name on the dish so they will know to whom to return it, or use disposable dishes. If you cannot deliver the food yourself, ask a Christian neighbor if they can.

Share recipes that are sugar-free, salt-free, fat-free, or have an extraordinary amount of vitamins/minerals. You could make a point to look through cookbooks to gather up a collection. Then you or a friend could type them up for a little booklet to be distributed or left on a table for people to pick up. Or you may wish to put a 5x7 recipe card on the church bulletin board for people to copy, and change it once a week.

Have someone in your home for a meal. Do this as often as possible. In so many homes these days, both husband and wife and working out of the home, and have so little time to have company. Hospitality is mentioned over and over as a sign of a good Jew or a good Christian throughout the Bible. Invite newcomers, new Christians, old friends, college students, service people, foster children, elders, senior citizens, people in nursing homes, just anyone you can think of. The meal does not have to be elaborate. You may invite two or three ladies for a late breakfast, or two or three widowed friends for lunch, or a family for a picnic in the backyard. It is hard to get out of the rut of inviting the same old friends all the time, but is worth it and a great blessing to everyone.

Whenever possible, invite more than one person or family at a time. This will not only help you get to know them better, but it will help your guests get to know each other better too. Try to invite families who know each other as acquaintances only, so a closer friendship can be developed. No telling how many lifetime Christian friendships you can encourage in your home.

If you do any baking *en masse*, the church may wish to write to a flour company and sugar company and tell them that you are using their product for charity work, and ask if there would be a way you could obtain their product at a discount or even as a donation. Again, as with yard goods, this company can write these off in their income tax, so you could possibly be doing them a favor too.

Send cookies to college students and service people whom you know of away from home. Even some county jails will accept cookies for inmates if you know of anyone in jail who needs encouragement. The cookies may go fast once they arrive, but the blessings will last and last. One of the best ways to pack those being mailed long distance is to freeze them first, then put them in a plastic bag, and surrounded them with popcorn. This should keep them both fresh and crumble free.

And, as with those who sew, if you know of a young married woman who does not know how to cook very well, invite her over and ask her if she would like to cook some things for some people with you. Then at the same time you could teach her some basic recipes. If you do very much baking for others, you probably don't use very complicated recipes. When you do teach another, you don't necessarily have to let her know that you know she can't cook. Cook with her as a partner, not as a master. And, by the way, more young men are "batching" until they get their career going before settling down, and would love some pointers and practical recipes.

Now let's talk about what the men can do for the homebound, seniors, handicapped, etc. Their homes need to be safe and vehicles running properly.

Do any of them in your congregation need grab bars installed in their bathroom by tub and toilet? Is there a small fire extinguisher in their kitchen near their stove and do they know how to use it? Are kitchen cupboards low enough they can he reached by an ever-shrinking senior? Are heating and air conditioning working properly? Are they able to change their air vents and how often? Who changes their light bulbs when they go out? Does their bed frame need to be lowered? Do they need handrails installed in their bathroom? How about in their bedroom in case they have to get up during the night? Are there nightlights in every room? Are batteries up to date in smoke detectors? Are handle-type door knobs needed to replace round door knobs that are too difficult to turn with arthritic hands? Do they have a peek hole in outside doors and are they low enough? Do they have a constant drip in a faucet or the toilet that needs adjusted or replaced? Do doors and windows fit snuggly against the cold or heat outside? Are there electronics in the home that need to be either fixed or disposed of?

If they have a car, are there any men available to check the air in the tires, oil level, condition of belts, strength of the battery? Can someone turn their motor on and look at the gauges to see if anything needs attention?

What about the outside of the house? Do they have a TV antenna that needs stabilized? Are the rain gutters free of leaves and other debris? Do they have a fence that is falling down in one place? Do they find climbing steps more and more difficult and need a ramp to get into their house? Do they have shutters coming loose and need nailed back up or a broken birdbath that needs disposed of? Has it been forty years since their house was painted? Could that be remedied? Are there trees that are unstable, might fall in a storm, and need to be taken down? Are there thick bushes hiding entrances from people on the sidewalk or neighbors and luring criminal intruders?

Perhaps the men of your congregation would like to create a sign-up sheet by categories: Carpentry, plumbing, electrical, and so on with as many sub-categories as they wish to include. A second sign-up sheet could be made for widows, shut-ins, and the handicapped with their name crossed off when their need has been filled. Be careful with this however, that able-bodied people do not sign up or people with families nearby who could do the work. Remember, I Timothy 5:3-10:

3 Give proper recognition to those widows who are really in need. 4 But if a widow has children or grandchildren, these should learn first of all to put their religion into practice by caring for their own family and so repaying their parents and grandparents, for this is pleasing to God. 5 The widow who is really in need and left all alone puts her hope in God and continues night and day to pray and to ask God for help. 6 But the widow who lives for pleasure is dead even while she lives. 7 Give the people these instructions, so that no one may be open to blame. 8 Anyone who does not provide for their relatives, and especially for their own household, has denied the faith and is worse than an unbeliever.

9 No widow may be put on the list of widows unless she is over sixty, has been faithful to her husband, 10 and is well known for her good deeds, such as bringing up children, showing hospitality, washing the feet of the Lord's people, helping those in trouble and devoting herself to all kinds of good deeds.

If families are nearby and neglecting their loved one, perhaps a letter could be sent to that family explaining their relative's needs. Sometimes those in need are afraid to "bother" their families. Many relatives just do not think of these things needing to be done.

There are other things men enjoy doing as a hobby that could bless others. Do you make woodworking knick-knacks, ceramics, dolls, macramé, etc.? Many people with such talents find themselves making so many they end up wondering what to do with them all, and perhaps finally put them in the top of a closet. Let the teachers of the Bible classes know they are available for awards or birthday presents. Are you good at making or repairing household items? If there is a storage room available, work could be done ahead of time to help people who have been hit by disaster such as fire or tornado or financial setback.

If you have access to some older furniture, you can take the old finish off and put a new one on to make them look practically like new. You could help develop a stored supply of basic items such as a sofa, kitchen table, a few chairs, a few beds, a dresser, dishes, silverware, linens. Whatever you can store, this will someday be a blessing to some family in the midst of crisis to give them a feeling of home and rest and dignity.

Can you repair toys and make them look like new? Can you create toys out of blocks of wood, pieces of rug, yard goods, buttons, and what-nots? You could send these toys to children's homes and foster homes. You could give a few to people receiving help with clothing or furniture. You could make them available to the Bible school teachers for awards or birthdays. Jesus loved the little children. He still does - through you.

Do you like to carve things out of wood? Someone can probably pick up a large supply of small board ends from construction sites, cabinet shops, school wood shops, etc. that would otherwise be burned. Recycle these into sheep, houses, trees, anything that could remind us of God's wonderful world.

Using a combination of craft skills, you could make a Bible-times village. Or a replica of the temple grounds; i.e., buildings, furniture, altars, tapestries, priests' clothing. Or you could make a dollhouse to be used for application stories in the younger Bible classes. Are you artistic? Make greeting cards from plain typing paper, and at the bottom of the pictures write, "Painted with love especially for you by your friend _____." Then leave the inside of the card blank and send personal messages to some of those people mentioned in the letter-writing chapter. Or you could give them to your Christian friends who cannot afford to purchase but send a lot of notes and cards.

Or you could make bulletin board cutouts to be used in various classrooms or a large one in your church foyer. Occasionally there may be a need for a drawing for your church bulletin to get across a certain point or advertise a coming special event.

You could make yourself available to teachers to create simple Bible application crafts for the children, or for flip charts for songs. A sign-up sheet could be set up so you would know when teachers needed materials and they could get with you to explain what they need. Or you could go through the Bible and select basic children's lessons always taught at some time and create teaching materials to be kept in a teachers' supply room or sent to missionaries. Also, there may be some Bible supply publishers who would like to publish your creations.

There are many things you can do at home. And an additional blessing is that your family and neighbors who drop by will see you will be able to see Christianity at work. If you have children watching you, perhaps they could help you a little, thereby learning to do Christian works and see how much fun it is at their impressionable age. Or friends and relatives stopping by to see you might be encouraged to join you. The old-fashioned quilting bees and house raisings were fun as well as a blessing, and you could end up with something similar at your kitchen table or garage.

One way or another, others who see you will learn and be blessed by your example. Yes, things in your home are not just things. They are hidden blessings just waiting for an opportunity to fly to the waiting hearts and lives of others.

9 ~ KEEPING YOUR HOME

This chapter is partly for women or men who choose not to be employed outside of their home to help make the living. You may be a stay-at-home dad or mom. But there are many things the career men and women can apply also. It is about keeping up your house, your home. If you have trouble keeping the clutter out and getting things done, this chapter is lovingly for you. If you find housework uncreative and unexciting, try this new and different approach. It just may work.

Yes, this IS a Christian work. But you may object right off that there are too many other Christian works to do, too many other people who really need you. You could even use this book Is proof. Right? Wrong. You could try to use the Bible as proof, using Jesus' rebuke to Martha for complaining that Mary wouldn't help her in the kitchen. Right? Sorry. Let's just look at it again.

As Jesus and his disciples were on their way, he came to a village where a woman named Martha opened her home to him. She had a sister called Mary, who sat at the Lord's feet listening to what he said. But Martha was distracted by all the preparations that had to be made. She came to him and asked, "Lord, don't you care that my sister has left me to do the work by myself? Tell her to help me!" "Martha, Martha," the Lord answered, "you are worried and upset about many things, but only one thing is needed. Mary has chosen what is better, and it will not be taken away from her" (Luke 10:38-42).

Two things indicate that Martha was in charge of this house. First, Martha was the one who did the welcoming; second, it was specifically referred to as her house. So, this means that Martha was primarily responsible for seeing that things were prepared for Jesus, their guest, and possibly also his apostles. This indeed would require a great deal of preparation. Nowhere in the Bible is a woman condemned for such preparations; but rather is praised for it. What, then, is the issue?

Martha finally went to Jesus and complained that she had to do all this serving [a good work] by herself, without her sister's help. This word "work" is sometimes translated "serve" and comes from a Greek word meaning to obey the commands of another; to do certain good things voluntarily. Examples are when a person becomes a Christian, a deacon ministers, the needy are helped, the hungry are fed. So Martha, in her statement, was indicating that what she was doing was a beneficial obligation to ensure the comfort of others. Is this what Jesus was condemning?

Martha's own interpretation of what she was doing, and Luke's inspired interpretation of what she was doing differ widely. If what she was doing was limited to serving, this would be in tune with the other teachings in the Bible. In fact, did not Jesus at another time state, *If anyone wants to be first, he must be the very last, and the servant of all* (Mark 9:35b)? Luke says Martha was "distracted." This word comes from a Greek word meaning to bustle about aimlessly, to busy oneself about trifling, needless, useless matters; used of a person who is meddlesomely inquisitive about others' affairs, a busybody; one who wanders around. This same "distracted" word used for Martha was also used in the following scriptures. *We hear that some among you are idle. They are not busy; they are busybodies* (1 Thessalonians 3:11). Besides, they get into the habit of being idle and going about from house to house. *And not only do they become idlers, but also gossips and busybodies, saying things they ought not to* (1 Timothy 5:13).

So then, when the Bible states that Martha was "distracted by all the preparations," it is emphatically referring to her undisciplined wandering around the kitchen doing needless things and not really doing any work, not accomplishing anything, and possibly even making matters worse. Martha was just spinning her wheels. Perhaps she was ashamed and embarrassed that she couldn't seem to get anything accomplished, so she put the blame on her sister.

Jesus lovingly chided, "Martha, Martha, you are worried and upset about many things." The word "worried" comes from a Greek word meaning to be drawn in different directions. The word "upset" comes from a Greek word meaning confusion. Another way of saying it would be, "Martha, you are going in every direction at once, all confused about so many things, and not getting anything done anyway. Come sit down with your sister and me." Jesus was definitely not condemning Martha for doing her housework or serving, but for wandering around getting nothing done, and using it as an excuse to not do important things.

It is all centered around attitude, point of view. Do you consider yourself a slave to your house or the queen of your house? If you do not have to go outside of your home to work, you have not only a spiritual obligation here, but a wonderful privilege and opportunity that men do not have. They go out and earn money - cold, hard cash. They may or may not earn it doing a job they like or feel a personal interest in. And what's it all for? Food, clothing, a comfortable and attractive home, And you, Your Majesty, king or queen of your house, you have the honor and privilege of turning that cold cash into those things s/he is earning the money for - making them a reality. That's the fun part!

However, you may feel that you are too much of a Martha, you seem to work all day and don't get anything done. You may ask, "Why try?" Below are some easy and uncomplicated ways to perform your good works in your home. With these suggestions you probably will think of others. So, your majesty, if you are ready for a suggestion, let us begin!

First, let's create a family for you. Let's assume you have four children ~ two school age and two preschool-age; and that your husband or wife must leave for work no later than 7:00 AM.

You will want to get up at 6:00 so as to avoid a rush. Now there isn't anything so bad about getting up at 6:00 if you go to bed at 10:00 - eights hours sleep. You can arrange for a half-hour nap during the early afternoon to get more sleep to refresh yourself halfway through the day. Or if it's purely a psychological hang-up, pretend you are living five time zones away and it is really 11:00 AM!

Before you ever leave your bedroom, you should get dressed, fix your face and hair - which shouldn't take more than twenty minutes if you're not going anywhere. Then tidy up your room - make your bed (not more than 3 minutes) and pick up clothes and other miscellany (about 5 minutes) ~ yes, including your husband's or wife's clothes. How wonderful! It is now 6:30 and you already have one room clean and yourself fresh and pretty, ready to be presented to your awakening family!

At 6:30 wake up your children. Call them only once. If they do not get up after the first call, this means you have indirectly trained them to stay in bed by letting them get by with it. So discipline them immediately (not yelling though, for you have a gentle voice ~ Proverbs

31:26), and retrain them. Unless you serve pancakes or waffles, it should not take you more than 15 minutes to fix sausage and eggs or oatmeal or something similar, with toast. Have your school-age children come into the kitchen and set the table for you.

At 6:45 the entire family should sit down to eat together. Remember, your husband is the king, your wife is the queen of the house. To start the day together as a family with your king at the end of the table will give a real feeling of closeness to your family and a warm sense of why and for whom your husband or wife is faithfully going to work every day. Do not ever let him or her eat alone - even if he claims he does not mind, for s/he probably would not let his pride admit it bothers them. Let them know s/he is special enough for the whole family to want to get up in time to be with them, and s/he'll think of you all through the day - really! What a wonderful good work this is!

Now it is 7:00 and everyone says goodbye to the man of the house. Your preschool children probably will still be dabbling at their plates. Your school-age children can now take up to half an hour to get dressed.

At 7:30 they should be ready to tidy up their own room - make their own bed, pick up their clothes, and put away their toys. Everything should be off the floor but the furniture. Nothing should be on the furniture but lamps and a few decorative items. If they do not have a toy box, give them a cardboard box to put in their closet or under their bed. If they do not have enough drawer or closet space for all their clothes, give them a box for socks and underwear to put in their closet or under their bed. But do insist that nothing be left out - no gum wrappers, no blocks, no doll shoes, no car tires.

You must discipline yourself and them to take care of everything. They should tell you when they are done so you can check. If anything is left out, point them out, then let them take care of that. If they are having trouble sticking with their chore, you may wish to set a kitchen timer to limit them to perhaps 20 minutes to clean up everything. For, like Martha, learning not to "fiddle around" is part of learning to be neat and clean.

When they are finished, compliment them and tell them their

room looks very nice. Brag on their accomplishment to both them and others within their hearing. They will feel good inside and will inspire others. They will also learn to stick with a job and not be quitters - a gift from you that will be valuable throughout their life. And for this, too, they will rise up and call you blessed.

During the time between 7:00 and 8:00 when your children are getting ready for school (this will have to be adjusted, of course, if they leave earlier), your preschool children can finish eating and then play while you wash the dishes and clean up the kitchen. If one or both of your preschoolers is above age two, they can be taught to carefully take most everything off the table for you. No child is too young to learn to help; and if you call them your good little helpers often, they will have a good feeling inside for being just like grownups.

To make your kitchen look as nice as possible, no matter how the woodwork or Formica or linoleum look, do not leave things sitting on your countertops, stovetops, and table that you can find a place for in your cabinets unless they are used often such as canisters. It should not take more than ten minutes to wash your breakfast dishes and another ten to dry them and put them away out of sight. Five minutes to wipe off the countertops, table and stovetops, ten minutes to sweep the floor, and ten minutes to mop it.

Your kitchen will take approximately 45 minutes to fix up; however, you will be interrupted by wiping off little ones' mouths and checking the older ones' rooms, so you should allow yourself an hour. Once you have done this, you will have a gleaming kitchen which you should not have to re-enter until noon (unless you wash or iron, etc., in there).

Now it is 8:00. You have been up two hours and have been very busy. Your husband or wife is gone and your older children have just left for school. You now deserve a little break. Take out of the freezer the meat for the evening meal, then fix yourself a cup of coffee or glass of tea and sit down in a comfortable place. If you do not want to just sit and stare, play with your little ones or read a chapter from the Bible or inspirational book, or knit, or do whatever else would relax you. But be careful not to start something that will be hard to tear yourself away from, such as a novel ~ it's taboo and for later. If your little ones bathe in the morning, they may wish to play in the tub during your half-hour rest, depending on their age.

At 8:30 take your little ones to their room to get dressed and do their share of cleaning up their room. If they are two, they are old enough to learn to make their own bed. Help them with it, but do not do it alone for them. Sure, it will take more time, but they will love doing things together with Daddy or Mommy, and love you all the more.

Sit down somewhere in their room, then, while they pick up their toys and clothes. If they are old enough to get them out, they are old enough to put them back. Then explain to them that throughout the day, whatever they get out to play with, when they are done they are to put it away before they get something else out to play with. You will have to have a lot of self-discipline to make this rule; but it's the only way to keep a clutter-free house.

Proverbs 19:18 tells us *Chasten your son while there is hope, and let not your soul spare for his crying* (KJV). *Train a child in the way he should go, and when he is old he will not turn from it* (Proverbs 22:6). It should not take more than 5 minutes to dress each child, and about 20 minutes to tidy up their room. Total, 30 minutes.

Now it is 9:00 and you have most of your house clean and tidy already! How wonderful, your majesty. You'd make anyone proud ~ including yourself. Don't you feel good? Isn't the world a wonderful place to live in? Haven't you already made your world a wonderful place to live in?

Go into your living room or den. This room should require the least amount of your time. The previous evening your children should have put their books, shoes and toys in their room. Therefore, all that may be in the living room or den in the morning is newspapers and perhaps dishes from an evening snack. If you knit or work on any project here, make sure there is a basket or someplace to put it away. It should not take you more than ten minutes to straighten it up and quickly dust. You still have time to sort dirty clothes and put your first load in. (With a family of six, doing two loads a day will keep things manageable.)

9:30 and you are ready to clean up the bathroom. Try your best to keep it odor-free and sanitary. Clean out the sink, tub, and toilet daily so they are never really a hard chore. Be sure to clean around the bases of these appliances where bacteria usually grow the most quickly. Then spray with a disinfectant. You will have fewer colds in your family doing this. Wipe off the mirror and chrome fixtures with window cleaner to make them really shine.

Put out of sight as many toiletries as possible to avoid clutter. If you do not have enough room in your medicine cabinet for everything, you might make yourself a little shadow-box type shelf on another wall in the bathroom, stain or paint the outside, and then for a door use an inexpensive framed picture hinged to your box on one side.

Last, mop the floor with some kind of sanitizing agent. This is extremely important to both cleanliness and health. It shouldn't take you more than half an hour to clean up your bathroom, and put your second load of clothes in the washer.

10:00 and Eureka! You're done! Amazing! And you've earned another rest. Pour yourself a hot or cold drink and sit down and relax awhile. Play with your children or read to them or whatever is relaxing and fun to you.

You have two hours left in your morning. Try to keep it as free of prior commitments as possible. Two or three times during the week you could use this time to do some major cleaning item such as vacuum, wash windows, clean cobwebs, or whatever. Or you could sew. Or if it is summer, you might want to work in your yard. There's lots of projects around the house to choose from.

If you don't need to do anything like that, sit down and write a letter to a family member who lives far away or one of the others mentioned in the chapter on letter writing in this book. You may wish to use this time to telephone people regarding personal, social or business matters, or to just encourage some friends. Or this may be your day to go to a Ladies Bible Class often held at 10:00, or some special club.

A word about avoiding clutter the rest of the day. Train yourself to give a room the once-over quickly whenever you enter or leave it to see if anything is sitting out that should not be ~ a cup, a toy, jewelry, a letter, a scarf. Pick it up and slip it into its place ~ about a 30-second job. This may sound picky, but you will save yourself a longer chore later, thus doing yourself a big favor. You now have until 3:30 or whenever your children get home from school to do the things you'd probably rather be doing ~ 5 or 6 hours. Have a wonderful day!

Make sure you are home when your school children arrive home from school. This gives them security, warmth and feelings of love. But, alas, you will have to keep clutter in the living room under control. There the coats are flung, the books are dropped, the shoes are taken off. Children should be trained to walk a few steps further and put these things where they'll be out of the way - hooks on the wall, in the closet, or even a doorknob. You may want to fold clothes (with a little ironing and mending thrown in?) while they tell you what all they did at school. Mostly just enjoy your children during this time. Make their homecoming special.

Begin dinner about an hour before you expect your husband or wife home if possible. Make sure the TV, etc. are turned down upon his arrival, for after all, s/he's had a very long day. Do try to make it peaceful ~ at least the first few minutes s/he is home. Greet at the door. If s/he was not trained while growing up to hang up their coat when s/he comes in, do not expect them to start now ~ just take that extra minute and hang it up for them with a smile and a prayer of thanksgiving that you have a husband or wife to come home to you and your children. Take the lunch pail or briefcase even before s/he drops it, and put it away. Then sit down at your table together. When your children are grown and gone, meal times together will be one of the happiest memories each of you will have.

After dinner, there is no reason why your school-age children should not divide up the duties and clean up the kitchen while you go into the living room or den with your husband to relax for the rest of the evening.

"But I still hate housework," you might declare after all this. "I know it's supposed to be noble and all that, and it is my Christian obligation, but to me it's nothing but plain drudgery and demeaning. Besides, I've got other more creative and satisfactory things to do."

Dear King or Queen, remember God is against confusion (1 Corinthians 14:33) and for order (1 Corinthians 14:40). He uses dirt as a symbol of sin (Isaiah 57:20) and cleanliness as a symbol of righteousness (Psalm 51:10). God uses bad odors as a punishment (Isaiah 3:24) and sweet smells as representative of sweet sacrifices (Philippians 4:18). Spots and blemishes represent the wicked, while white is pure and good (Isaiah 1:18).

Noble Lord or Lady of your palace, if you like creativity, then create! And since God uses symbolism, you use symbolism too. Use creative symbolism. Here's how:

Look at those dirty dishes. Wash each one as though it were a jewel in your heavenly crown to be made bright again. Look at the marks and dirt on your floor. Sweep it and mop it and put a little shine on it to give yourself and your family a little foretaste of the clean and shining streets of gold you will walk on in the heavenly realm. Look at your dirty oven. Wash it even as the Lord washes away your sins.

Look at those wrinkled clothes. Iron each piece as a work of art to see how smooth and silk-like you can make them for your royal household. Look at those torn clothes. Mend them as the Lord mends hearts when they are torn and broken.

Look at your dirty windows. Wash them and let the golden sunshine into your home, your life, your heart. Look at your messy bed. Pull the sheets and covers up nice and smooth, and then crown it with a bedspread the color of a gem from the very foundation of your heavenly home.

Yes, everything you do can remind you of the royal home that is awaiting you in heaven, and the royal realm of the home that is all your own, and with which your Lord has so greatly blessed you. Whatever you do, work at it with all your heart, as working for the Lord (Colossians 3:23).

You are the only one in your little world who can make your home into your family's fortress and palace. You are the only one, dear Christian Lord or Lady, dear father or mother, dear husband or wife, who is truly worthy (Proverbs 31) to do this for them. God bless you in this truly worthy good work that is as great as you are!

10 ~ IN THE WORKPLACE

The Bible talks of both men and women having careers. We know less of the women though. Many were employed at something away from home either because of financial need or because they were needed in the community. This chapter will cover what both men and women can do on the job as Christian examples. But first, a few paragraphs regarding occupations women held in the Bible.

Briefly, in the realm of working with their hands, we have the examples of Hagar the maid (Genesis 16), Rahab the innkeeper (Joshua 2), Ruth the farm worker (Ruth), a maid (2 Kings 5), Rhoda another maid (Acts 12) and Priscilla a tent maker (Acts 18).

Professional women in the Bible include midwives (Exodus 1:15), Jochebed a nurse (Exodus 2 and 6), Deborah a judge (Judges 4), Vashti and Esther both queens (Esther), the worthy woman who invested in real estate and retailing (Proverbs 31), and Lydia a merchandiser of purple (Acts 16).

Did any of these women do anything unusual in the course of their employment to make them stand out? Hagar started showing up her employer, Sarah, and bragging about it, until Sarah finally fired her (Genesis 16). Rahab, an innkeeper, used her facilities to harbor people who were trying to stand up for right in antagonistic society (Joshua 2). Ruth needed a job, so went to a possible place of employment where she worked hard and had a good attitude. She did not get hired, but did end up marrying the boss (Ruth).

A maid was concerned about her employer's health and told him who may be able to help (2 Kings 15). Rhoda had a menial task seemingly, but on the day that it could have been the highlight of her life, she got too excited and didn't carry out her part of the work (Acts 12). Priscilla helped her husband in their business and in the process met and assisted someone who was able to influence countless others to do right - Paul (Acts 18).

Some nurses (midwives) were told to do things that were morally wrong, and risked their lives to stand up for right (Exodus 1:15). Jochebed kept herself aware of the problems of a high government official so that when someone was needed to do a job for which she was qualified, she was already there and available (Exodus 2).

Deborah became a judge during a time when the rest of the government was so corrupt a foreign country controlled much of it. She was finally able to get some of the men to stand up for right and a godly nation was reborn (Judges 4). Vashti, the wife of the head of state, was expected to be immoral for the sake of showing the superiority of her nation; but she left her position rather than compromise her ethics (Esther 1).

Esther, too, was the wife of the head of state. Her husband became the unwitting pawn of the politically corrupt, and she risked execution to reveal the plot to him (Esther). A certain woman balanced a home and career in real estate and retailing in such an admirable way that both she and her husband were known and welcomed into the company of the city leaders (Proverbs 31). Lydia merchandised purple cloth and developed a sizeable company. She had such influence over her employees that they went to worship with her (Acts 16).

First we will discuss what the EMPLOYEES can do. Employees primarily include office staffs, maintenance people, salespeople, and people in the services such as nurses, teachers, etc. Some of these suggestions are obvious, but hopefully there will be some new ideas here for you.

You can do as much of a variety of good works among the people with whom you work as with fellow Christians. If someone stays home from work sick, you can call and see how they're doing (during break time, please). Ask if they need anyone to stop by the drug store for them. Stop by to see them if they are on your way home from work. Buy a get well card to send them.

If they are going to be out a week or so and no one else at your job does, pass around a card for everyone to sign and send that. It would depend on how long you have worked there, how long the person was going to be out sick, and what office or shop policy may be whether someone started a flower fund; but whoever starts it, be sure to chip in and do your share.

If the person goes to the hospital, try your best to go see them as much as possible. If most of their friends are "working people" who have very little time for themselves and their families, your sick coworker probably will not get many visits and your extra effort will mean that much more. This may be your opportunity to tell them God will take care of them. Do not hesitate to tell them you are praying for them. You might also ask them if they would like a minister to come by and see them, and that yours would be happy to. If they begin responding to you about religion, let them talk. Reflect back to them what they are saying, such as....

"I haven't been to church in a long time."

"You seem to miss it."

"Yeah, I was always so busy on weekends catching up with my housework, you know."

"Oh yes, I know all about that! It's hard getting up early enough for church. But I'm always glad I did afterward." "Sometimes I miss things like that."

"Have you thought about going back?"

"Sometimes, but usually I'm too tired."

"When you get to feeling better, would you like to go with me? If Sunday is a problem, you could go on Wednesday evening. Want to give it another try? Which would be a better day for you?"

Another situation that you will occasionally run in to in your work are people with family funerals. It's startling the number of people who do not have church affiliation anymore. If someone takes off work for a funeral, you know it is for a close relative. Be sure to send a sympathy card to their home. You may wish to call them the evening after the funeral and ask them how they are doing, if you are fairly close to them. They may say that funerals are frustrating to them and they don't like to go and don't like to talk about it. Or they may tell you how many people were there, how things were at the cemetery, and so on.

You may ask how the immediate family has been taking it. There will be different responses to this. It is likely to lead to difficult questions that they may be searching for someone to answer for them. There will be questions such as, "If God is so good, why does he allow suffering and death?" Such questions are dealt with in the chapter on "Loss of Loved Ones" and Appendix C.

Depending on how close they were to the one who died, they may need someone to talk to. Visiting them in their home and having them in your home to get them away from the reminders of their loss temporarily are thoughtful gestures. You may kind of keep an eye on them at work to see whether they are able to concentrate or if they rush off to the restroom suddenly. Depending on them and the situation, you may wish to go to them and quietly give them a hug and tell them you'll say an extra prayer for them. If they seem to need extra time off at lunch, it may be possible to ask your supervisor if you could work through your lunch hour in place of that person. And if you know part of their job, you could try to do some of their work for them.

Of course at such times people are thinking of their own eternal destiny, are searching, and are open to teaching and going to church more than at any other time of life. Do not pass up any opportunity to encourage them and teach them.

Is someone engaged or going to have a baby? Again, depending on your office, how long you've been there, etc., the office may want to have a "Jack-and-Jill" shower. The shower may be on a lunch hour or it may be in a home. Women are especially adept at giving this kind of party/shower. You may wish to make it simple with a gift and card on their desk during break, or stay after work an hour and have something in a conference room. But be sure to have something.

If, for some reason, the others are not interested in doing anything for this person, that is all the more reason for you to. They may not be very popular, or they may be too new, or she was told to get an abortion and refused, or whoever they're going to marry nobody likes. Whatever the situation, they have announced that they are going through with things and may need all the moral support possible. In such case, if you are a woman you could take them out to lunch if you can afford it. Or you would buy a little something and give it to them before or after work.

If a year later, for instance, they decide they made a mistake choosing their spouse, you may be the only one they feel comfortable talking with; they definitely wouldn't go to the "I-told-you-so's."

How about your fellow employees? Do they tend to gossip? Gossip can be defined as talking about any situation of a person not present that is negative and uncomplimentary. Gossip does not necessarily have to be false. Also it does not necessarily have to be something that is unkind; it may be about the trouble someone is having with a relative. A safe rule is to not say anything about a person unless it is obviously complimentary.

If there is a compliment, save it for when the person is with the group and give them an audience for the compliment. This sometimes helps keep gossip under control. If someone in your group does begin to gossip, very subtly change the subject. You do not have to embarrass anyone by pointing out the error of their way in front of the others. You could change the subject by complimenting someone in your group and talking about that.

Is there ever a time when telling something negative about a person not present is not gossip? A general rule of thumb would be to only tell it to someone who could be of assistance. And even then make your conversation short to eliminate the temptation to be judgmental.

All the above has been devoted to good works to reflect the love of God to those with whom you work. These are things that atheists might also do but just to show their love, not God's love. Therefore, whenever you do something kind and someone expresses appreciation, you might say something like, "Well, I feel I have been blessed with a pretty good life and just wanted to pass it on." They may look at you strangely for such a statement, but they'll store it away in their minds until such a time they feel a need to find out why you've been blessed and how they can have such a life. You'd be surprised how many times this works.

Now we come to a work that not only shows the love of God in this world, but his desire to extend that love on into eternity. It may be that you could start a Bible study with one or more of those with whom you work. The suggestions following would apply in part to studies in your home, but will be directed more specifically to the work environment.

One day when you mention God's blessings casually (please don't talk about God much though), someone will ask you a question. It is likely to be a hard question, a challenging question about how God has let them down. Or it may really have nothing to do with the Bible, but they think it does, such as, "Yeah, idleness definitely is the devil's workshop." This is your opportunity to respond with a suggestion such as this:

"You know, I'd like to know more about that too. Let's get together and do some research on that. How about on our lunch hour next Thursday?"

You do not have to make it sound like a long-term situation. If you plan it that way and it fizzles out, you could become too discouraged to try again later. But if you plan for something temporary to just answer a few questions and fill some curiosities about the Bible, and then later the group decides it wants to keep meeting, that's like a bonus.

At first, however, you will not have a group. Start with one person. Once that person says they'd like to do something like that once or for a couple weeks, you might add, "Do you think any of the others would like to come? Should we keep it just the two of us or let anyone join us who wants to?" Unless your friend is shy or would be embarrassed by thinking s/he knows less about the Bible than anyone else, s/he will probably agree to invite others, and may get excited about it. When you approach the others, be casual and say something like, "Hey, Joe and I are going to get together in the conference room next Tuesday, eat our lunches together, and look up some things in the Bible we're curious about. Want to join us? Got anything about the Bible your curious about and want to look up?

For your studies you should bring the same version of Bible if possible. Also bring a small paperback concordance to look up the main word describing a topic and find all the scriptures listed which include that word. With a concordance you can look up anything and get God's complete point of view on that subject. Options may include something like a *Halley's Bible Handbook* in paperback, giving a brief description of each book in the Bible and some archaeological discoveries. Probably everyone should have a note pad to write down the gist of each passage so a conclusion can be drawn easier, especially if there are many scriptures to look up. If someone brings up something that you know is about a very personal problem, discuss it briefly if there are others present and then ask in private if s/he'd like to study that topic with you alone, even if it's at home in the evening over the telephone.

If this develops into a long-term situation, you should eventually bring in to the discussion studies of how first-century people became Christians so you can all make sure you have followed or will follow the same example.

Now back to your desk and back to work station. Under no circumstance should you compromise your ethics. In some company cultures, people are expected to say certain unchristian phrases, lie at certain times, take home some of the office or shop supplies, drive the company car for personal use, etc. In many cases you can work around a problem so that you can handle the situation satisfactorily and do not have to compromise your standards. In such a case, you will be an example for good to those around you, because they will definitely notice it. In other cases, you may not be able to work around it. You may prefer to go to your supervisor and just say, "I just can't do it that way. Is there some other way I can accomplish the same thing?" Many times the supervisor will appreciate what you are saying; if they don't, you don't want to work there. Even if your standards may be higher than theirs, often they respect that, they definitely will learn you can be trusted, and sometimes that leads to company opportunities for you.

Up to this point we have been primarily concerned with what you as a Christian employee can do with your fellow employees. However, something more should be mentioned about what you can do for your employer. Although the following passage refers to slaves and their relationships to masters, it still applies to the work situation. Therefore, we will substitute the word employees and employers:

Employees, obey your earthly employers with respect and fear, and with sincerity of heart, just as you would obey Christ. Obey them not only to win their favor when their eye is on you, but like employees of Christ, doing the will of God from your heart. Serve wholeheartedly, as if you were serving the Lord, not men, because you know that the Lord will reward everyone for whatever good he does, whether he is the employee or the employer (Ephesus 6:5-8).

The primary concern of someone who has been hired to do a job should be to do whatever the employer needs done. Remember, the owner of the business is trying to earn a living, and needs the assistance of others to build the business up. It is not your money that they are giving you, but rather the business's money earned as a result of many people working together. You are receiving a portion of that. That is called wages. If you do not help in some way to earn more money for the business, you are taking wages you did not earn.

It may be that your job is to make sure the floors are clean; this can help the business by making a clean atmosphere for people to work in and customers to come to that otherwise would not go there. So whatever you do, you were hired to help build up the business. If you do not do your job but just show up to fill the time and collect your wages, you are stealing from your employer, taking their money without having earned it. Ecclesiastes tells us, *Whatever your hand finds to do, do it with all your might* (9:10a).

What if your employer is not kind to you? First, be sure they are not angry because you are having private conversations outside of break times, not doing your work, etc. You can take Paul's counseling to heart as we saw in Ephesians, and consider yourself working for Christ. If your employer or supervisor is so bad they seem to be your enemy, then consider what Jesus said in his Sermon on the Mount, to pray for those who despitefully use you (Matthew 5:434-48).

Truly we love others as we love ourselves. Therefore, you could help your employer or supervisor love themselves better by leaving a note on their desk of appreciation for what they are accomplishing. You can compliment them on their shoes, ask about the family, recognize their frustration occasionally with a "You're under a lot of pressure, aren't you?". Remember Paul's advice on how to relate to our enemies:

Bless those who persecute you; bless and do not curse....Do not repay anyone evil for evil. Be careful to do what is right in the eyes of everybody. If it is possible, as far as it depends on you, live at peace with everyone. Do not take revenge....Do not be overcome by evil, but overcome evil with good (Romans 12:14-21).

Be careful that you do not begin telling others about how unlikable this person is, for in the very process of doing that you become an unlikable person also. When you think about it, most people who treat others unkindly think they are just defending themselves. They do not think of themselves as the unkind person. Therefore, it is vital that you not let that cycle begin but rather speak only good of others, for your own well being as well as theirs.

Now we will discuss EMPLOYERS. Those of you reading this who are self-employed or who have hired people to assist you have some added opportunities. One opportunity is in the realm of advertising. Your business cards could be printed with a statement of your Christianity, or variation of a Bible verse such as "Do unto others as you would have them do to you."

You could advertise your company in the newspaper by saying you follow the golden rule. Or you could run an ad with a Bible verse applicable to current times and add your company name and service at the bottom. On the radio you could sponsor a spot such as a single Bible verse read, children singing a church song, or your minister saying a few words. Your contracts or stationery could refer to the golden rule.

Keep a Bible on your desk, even if you never read it there, not to show off but as a symbol of what guides your life and business. People will be able to tell the difference as to why it's there by your attitudes and language. Invite your employees to start out the day with you with a Bible reading, and a prayer asking God to be with everyone through the day. Have a different Bible verse on the bulletin board each week.

Contact the benevolent committee of your congregation telling them you would be willing to consider hiring any people who come to them for monetary assistance. People with financial problems are likely to have optimism problems, as discussed in the chapter on benevolence. You would need to work with them to develop their self-confidence and confidence in others. Keep your standards high and show such people how to lift themselves up to those heights.

In general treatment of employees, these Bible passages show ways to handle them. Where the word slave may appear, the word employee is substituted:

Do not take advantage of a hired man who is poor and needy....Pay him his wages each day before sunset, because he is poor and is counting on it (Deuteronomy 24:14,15). *Employers, treat your employees in the same way. Do not threaten them, since you know that he who is both their Master and yours is in heaven, and there is no favoritism with him* (Ephesians 6:9).

Yes, whatever your vocation, you are ultimately working for God, whether you are an employee or employer, whether you are a laborer or professional. Therefore, let us take Ephesians 4:1 and 2 and apply it to our work situation as Christians:

I beseech you that you walk worthy of the vocation wherewith you are called, with all lowliness and meekness, with longsuffering, forbearing one another in love (KJV). God be with you and shine forth from you to those with whom you work.

11 ~ CHURCH OFFICE

There was a time when the English word, "secretary," meant one who could keep the secrets of another. Then it came to mean one who could also assist in other ways. Today we have Secretary of State, Secretary of the Treasury, Secretary of Labor. For about a century we had private secretary, executive secretary, and just plain secretary. Today, because both men and women know and use computers, the late 21st-century job description of secretary, except in government, is almost obsolete. Now, we use the term Administrator.

The Bible uses both the word secretary and administrator. Nave's Topical Bible categorizes secretaries as scribes and transcribers of the law, the king's assistant, and the mustering officer in the army. The earliest notation of a secretary in the Bible is a list of King David's officers, including a man called his "recorder" and another man called his "secretary" (2 Samuel 8:16,17).

The term "administrator" is not found in the Bible, but administration is found in the New Testament. The Greek is *diakonia* from whence comes deacon or minister. I Corinthians 12:5-6 translates it different kinds of service....different kinds of working.

This is how Lyndon Johnson, one of the U.S. presidents, got his start in Washington, D.C. ~ as a secretary. The secretary to the chairman of the board of large corporations were always men. By the 1960s, and for about thirty years, only women were secretaries. Men began rejoining the ranks again in the 1990s. Administrators and secretaries have always been extremely important and they will continue to be as long as there is a need to develop, organize, carry out, and record important functions and events.

Today some mega-churches have administrators who work as treasurer, bookkeeper, etc. This chapter, however, is for the average size congregation. There are many ways today that you can help with the details of the good works that the church as a whole is trying to accomplish. Regardless of how menial some may seem at first, they are necessary and important. Without the little things, the larger things could not be accomplished. The smaller stones are the bedrock upon which the main structure is built.

Probably the most obvious thing a church office administrator takes care of is the church bulletin. We are not told in the Bible to have a church bulletin, but we are told to be concerned one for another and to encourage one another. The details and hows are left up to us, such as by telephone, automobile, or in this case by bulletin.

There are many ways to organize a bulletin. Most bulletins have the front page for a picture of the building, a listing of services, and/or an inspirational item. The second page has the news of who is ill, who is bereaved, what classes are having special activities, who is having a birthday, who had a baby, who got married, area-wide meetings, potluck dinners, etc. The third page usually has a special article written by the minister(s) or elder. And the last page usually is left at least half blank to facilitate mailing.

Often the selection of inspirational items is left up to whoever compiles the bulletin. You could make a collection in a 5x7 card file and categorize them by topic or put them in a database on your computer. You could also keep on hand books of inspirational articles and poems. You may find what the "editorial" article by the minister is going to be about each week, then include a poem, quotation, or whatever you have on the same topic to create a weekly theme.

There are various formats to use in arranging and typing a bulletin. For the greatest simplicity, you can just start at the top of the paper and type down to the bottom. Or you can turn your paper sideways (landscape in computerese) and type two pages separately on each half. When you are done with it, photocopy it, fold in the middle, and it comes out in book format. You could also make the page look more like a newspaper with two or three columns. Newspapers have learned that people can read faster and easier with narrower reading lines.

You should have some kind of headline at the first part of each separate news item. This way the readers will be able to pay special attention to those items that most concern them. All names in your news items should be underlined or in bold print. People like to read about people, and people like to see their names in print. This helps draw attention to those we need to know about.

If you have a postal permit from the post office, on the corner where stamps normally go, draw a square and inside it type, "POSTAL PERMIT NO. 68" or whatever your assigned permit number is. If you are mailing about 75 bulletins and putting first-class postage on each, you can probably get a much cheaper rate by increasing your mailing list to a minimum of 200 and getting a permit so you can mail at a fraction of the first-class rate. Check with your post office on all this.

Of all the administrative assistance you give, the bulletin will be the most time-consuming. But it is not actually that difficult once you get the hang of it. Just think of all the people who will receive an extra message of love from the bulletin, and will also receive information on the ill, bereaved, and others who need their help. So many good Christian works could be done if more people knew when someone needed them. The bulletin can help spread the word.

Whatever computer program you use, remember that you are licensed by the software company to use their software. If you copy what someone else has, you are using the software without paying for it, which is outright theft. So, let's be ethical with whatever programs the church uses. With a license, any time you have a problem or question, you can often call the company's 800 number for immediate assistance. This is much faster than spending hours trying to find the solution in the manual.

If you would like the capability of printing sharp photos without having to paste them onto your master, you can obtain a scanner for your computer. Just place the photo in the scanner, and it will take its own photo to put into your document. Photos will not reproduce well on black-and-white photocopiers. However, they print just like original photos on color-capable photocopiers. So, even if your photos are black and white, use a color-capable photocopier to make them clear and sharp.

Let's now consider the use of computers. Try to set up an email account for your congregation, even if you do not have regular office hours. Most email providers explain how you can do so for a small fee. Then list your congregation in the various church directories on the internet. Just be sure you keep your listings up to date.

On your computer, you can set up a "Scripture-a-Day Club" for your members and community. Use your imagination in collecting email addresses of people in your community. One idea is to join a community internet group, and as people send messages, you collect their email address.

You can create an internet "group" (mailing list) through Yahoo, Google, or other provider specializing in such service. To keep it simple for you. Or you can create a private Facebook page for the congregation.

In your welcome letter (which will be set up when you set up your group) explain this is only a short scripture and comments each day and not a discussion group. Also explain how they can unsubscribe if they do not wish to remain in your group.

Now and then you will receive feedback from people who appreciate reading the daily devotionals and asking if they could put them on their Facebook or other social media pages.

Does your congregation have a web site? The major search engines (Google, Yahoo, etc.) or private web providers offer webspace at a very reasonable rate ($10/mo) and provide telephone technical assistance in setting it up. It is now possible to set up a website without knowing technical codes. You can list your congregation's address and meeting times, monthly activities, etc. You can include pictures from your Vacation Bible School, teacher's workshop, clothing giveaway or whatever your congregation is involved in. You can place your weekly bulletin on it, and your monthly activity calendar. Of course you can then expand it to include Bible studies.

When you set it up, be sure to fill out the "tags" for each page. These are main words that explain what is on each page. That is what is collected by the search engines so your website comes up in the choices of people searching for that subject. Of course, the more pages and subjects you cover on your website, the more likely people are likely to find your website.

For the above reason, you might want to have a special page listing people and dates for births, marriages, and obituaries. These can be collected if your local newspaper is online. Then, when people use a loved one's name for an internet search, they will find your website.

If you cannot type or use a computer, you can help fold and address the bulletins. If they are not mailed to all the members of your congregation, there are always other churches and former members who want copies. You could be of great assistance in this.

Many congregations have cards for people to sign when they arrive at services so the elders can tell who was able to attend each week. With a hundred or more people, it is very difficult to notice everyone who was present.

We can follow up with those who were unable to attend, and see whether or not they were ill. So often someone is ill for a week or two and no one ever knows it. Or perhaps someone got upset over something someone said in a class, and may be on the brink of dropping out completely because of Misunderstanding. Or perhaps someone hasn't been to the assembly for months, and since they usually sit in the back and rush right out, we didn't realize they'd been absent so long. So many people drift away from the church unnoticed, and the reason is often because they feel exactly that: unnoticed and unneeded.

You could play an important part with those cards. You could put them in alphabetic order each week, mark those who were there, and take note of those who were not. Then you could pass them onto the elders so they can watch over the souls of everyone as carefully as possible. Hebrews 13:17 states, *They keep watch over you as men who must give an account.* Yes, our elders must give an account of what happens to the souls of everyone they are over, and you can help with this vital and grave responsibility.

Also, attendance cards have other information on them. Sometimes people write announcements on them, or request for prayers, or questions for preacher. Sometimes they request a private Bible study or a home visit. The cards will also tell whether the person is a member or visitor. All cards with any of this on them can be set aside and given to appropriate people to follow up with.

If you have cards for the visitors to sign, be sure to include a place for them to include their email on it. Also, instead of the standard "Guest of", you could ask, "How did you learn about this congregation?".

Does the congregation send out letters to the visitors to the services, new Christians, and new members in general? Would they if there was someone to type them? Perhaps your help is needed for this. There are so many good works left undone because no one knows anyone to do them. Do you ever have revivals or special lecture weeks where letters or fliers are mailed to everyone in the community? If so, volunteer to help stuff envelopes and seal them or fold and address flyers. This is a job that takes a while. But with several helping, it should not take long and is even rather enjoyable when done as a group.

When there is a Vacation Bible School, someone is needed to help register the little ones. This is one of the most effective ways there is of reaching out into the community. Every child's full name, grade, address, telephone number, and the names of parents need to be registered. Then an accurate record needs to be kept daily to see which children return. Whoever is absent you or the regular teacher can call and see if they need a ride.

At the end of the Vacation Bible School, the church as a whole or the individual teachers may wish to send a letter to each child and parent, inviting them to come on Sundays and/or Wednesdays also. Then a follow-up visit could be made by the Sunday school teacher. But records need to be kept so they will know whether to write and where to go when they visit. Again, this may seem like a small task, but it is very important for a good foundation for the growth and development of the Bible class.

Does your congregation help a missionary anywhere? Write and tell them you would be willing to help with their correspondence. Usually many different congregations and individuals take an interest in missionaries and send funds. Yet they are working so hard among the people that they rarely have the time to sit down and write letters except perhaps before breakfast or around midnight. Just being able to dictate letters on a tape recorder and send them to you for typing and mailing would be a tremendous service. You can work out something about the signature. Some missionaries ask that the letters be sent back to them for signatures and mailing. Others ask you to mail them out yourself directly. A lot would depend on whether it was a personal or business letter.

If you have several elders in your congregation and a lot of mail comes to them, they probably have a hard time getting all the correspondence sorted out in their minds. If you are a genuine "secretary" in the original sense and can keep SECRETS, perhaps they would be interested in your sending them photocopies of all the letters, and then typing out a one- or two-sentence summary of each letter all on one piece of paper to use as reference at their meetings. Often many of their letters are not answered because there is no one to help them get all the replies out. If you are one of the few people left who learned shorthand and remember some of it, tell the minister and elders you could take dictation once a week either in person or on the phone. However, most just type them on the computer themselves now.

Just remember, all their mail is strictly confidential and usually even their wives do not know about them. For their letters are from people needing help with their problems (what if the sordid news leaked out?), and from people needing financial assistance (what if people thought money was being spent that really wasn't?), and possible projects (what if people heard about a project that was later canceled?). So be prudent, keep their confidence, and help them in the process.

Is there a Christian children's home, nursing home, daycare center or social services organization near you? They survive on token charges for services if any, and donations of both money and time from people like you. They have many details that need to be taken care of and a great deal of paperwork. You could free those in charge of these programs to do the work for which they were chosen, instead of bogging themselves down in mires of paperwork.

Many letters requesting support go out. Often there is a monthly newsletter that is sent out to keep people informed of their ministry. They could use help with this. If their staff is really short-handed, you could help answer the telephone and/or be a receptionist on a volunteer basis. Help the administrators with routine correspondence if the need arises. Help file. Records must be kept straight or no one would know what was being done with whom or when. The organization may or may not have a secretary, but few ever have enough help.

In order to help your entire congregation be filled with "love and good works" (Hebrews 10:25), you might keep a card file or database categorizing various works that need to be done, either on a regular basis or periodically or on special occasions. Although Christians must do their good works whether or not someone else has asked them to, some occasions call for a larger coordination in order to accomplish a large-scale work. Each category would have sub-categories. Major tab headings might be as follows:

> Greeting Cards/Notes
> Benevolence
> Transportation
> Domestic
> Telephone
> Secretarial
> Visiting
> Hospitality
> Home Maintenance
> Car Maintenance
> Foreign Missions
> Special People
> Church Building Maintenance
> Bible Teaching
> Public Worship
> Leadership

An example of types of sub-categories or sub-tabs is:

TELEPHONE WORK

Call a shut-in daily
Call absentees on Monday
Call bus children every Saturday
Call members regarding unexpected events
Call new Christians daily to encourage

An explanation of the "Special People" category: This would be if a person wanted to concentrate on helping people such as senior saints, youth, overweight, drug abusers, alcohol abusers, singles, single again, deaf, blind, mentally handicapped, physically handicapped, ex-convicts, pre-schoolers, marriages, unemployed, etc.

By keeping such a file, you could help your congregation do its work as a group and avoid unintentionally neglecting any area.

You could make calling cards with the name and address of your congregation on it. You could add a line for them to fill in their name. Or, you could write at the top "courtesy of" with the congregation's name and address below. This could encourage members to do "random acts of kindness" in the community, and then give whoever they helped one of the calling cards. You can buy blank calling cards at most office supply stores.

Regardless of what you do in an administrative capacity, remember that whoever you are helping, you are a part of their work, you are a fellow worker with that person or those persons. God gave each one of us certain talents; and he expects us to use them or lose even that which we know how to do (Matthew 25:14-28). Above all, as you bless others with your help, you will receive a multiplied blessing in return. And isn't that wonderful!

12 ~ WORLDWIDE MISSIONARY

Jesus said in Mark 16:15 and 16, "*Go into all the world and preach the good news to all creation. Whoever believes and is baptized will be saved, but whoever does not believe will be condemned.*" Jesus did not say for some of us to go. He expects us all to do our part.

Twenty years from the time Jesus commanded this, it had been done. The whole world had received the Good News. How do we know this? Because the Bible tells us so!

Acts 17:6 quotes some local leaders declaring, *These men who have caused trouble all over the world have now come here.* The KJV reads, *These that have turned the world upside down are come hither also.* When Paul wrote the Roman Christians about six years before Nero burned Rome, he told them, "*First, I thank my God through Jesus Christ for all of you, because your faith is being reported all over the world.*" Later in his letter he defended the fact that the gospel has indeed gone to the whole world. *Did they not hear? Of course they did: Their voice has gone out into all the earth, their words to the ends of the world* (Romans 1:8; 10:18). And in another letter, Paul was just as explicit:

This is the gospel that you heard and that has been proclaimed to every creature under heaven, and of which I, Paul, have become a servant (Colossians 1:23b).

The Bible tells us that the Good News went out to the Orient or Far East (Matthew 2:1,2), the Middle East (Acts 2:9-11), Africa (Acts 8:27-39), and Europe (Acts 14-28). But how was that possible with only a nucleus of twelve men?

Acts 2 explains that on a day sometime after the selection of the apostle to take Judas' place (verse 1), the Holy Spirit gave a special gift to the twelve: All of them were filled with the Holy Spirit and began to speak in other tongues as the Spirit enabled them (verse 4). Yes, all of them were speaking with the Spirit's guidance, not just Peter. Verses 9 and 10 list all the people present who heard in their language, and when you add up the number of languages represented, there are about as many languages as apostles. We only know Peter's sermon, although there is indication that all the apostles spoke, possibly to various groups around the temple and probably to several hundred each. Then collectively the account tells of the people asking "Peter and the other apostles" what they should do to be saved.

Of course this gift was no surprise since it had been predicted for hundreds of years in the Old Testament in such places as Isaiah 28:11. *With foreign lips and strange tongues God will speak to this people. This being one of the signs of the apostles* (2 Corinthians 12:12), they gave this power to other Christians to help spread the Word to the whole world. (Some weaker Christians abused this and sometimes spoke these foreign tongues to people who did not speak them and did not understand them, just to show off. Christians in Corinth were among them.)

Because of this ability to speak in foreign languages not previously learned, the Christians of the first century were able to preach the gospel to the whole world. But what about us today? We have the "miracles" of radio, the printing press, airplanes, automobiles, world-wide mail, TV, the internet, etc. We are expected to use whatever resources are available to us.

True, our part of the world for us to convert begins with our own neighborhood. This in itself is an encouragement to foreign missionaries. E. Stanley Jones explained seventy years ago in his book, *The Christ of the Indian Road:*

I do not make a special drive upon you because you are the neediest people of our race, but because you are a member of our race. I am convinced that the only kind of a world worth having is a world patterned after the mind and spirit of Jesus. I am therefore making a drive upon the world as it is, in behalf of the world as it ought to be, and as you are a part of that world I come to you. But I would not be here an hour if I did not know that ten others were doing in the land from which I come what I am trying to do here. We are all in the same deep need. Christ, I believe, can supply that need.

So, yes, it is important that we begin to do missionary work in our own neighborhood. It is such a tremendous encouragement to foreign missionaries. It seems that the more people are interested in teaching people where they live, the more they become interested in what the foreign teachers are teaching where they live too. Kind of goes together.

Now, in what ways can we be fellow workers with teachers in other countries? Monetary support is one obvious way. Inflation in other countries is often much greater than our own, and it may take five times as much money to buy groceries as in our own country. Of course they need a house or apartment to live in and transportation, and clothing, and supplies and materials with which to teach. These all cost money. God can supply what they need through you.

Missionaries return to the states temporarily for various reasons: Add to their education, allow teenage children to go to a Christian school, raise funds, visit previous supporting congregations and friends, or just to have a good rest. They need someone to stay with if they don't have the money for motels or rent. You could be a fellow-worker with them by providing a place to stay whenever they are in your area.

Probably the most noted ones in the Old Testament to provide housing for a traveling preacher was a Shunammite couple. 2 Kings 4:8-10 tells how they added a room onto their house, and Elisha was to consider it his room whenever he was in the area. A Christian couple in the New Testament often cited as an example of having many godly qualities were Aquila and Priscilla. When Paul went to Corinth to live and preach for a little while, he stayed in their home (Acts 18:1-4), working at his occupation during the week and preaching on weekends. Of Aquila and Priscilla, Paul spoke in Romans 16:3 as "my fellow workers in Christ Jesus."

What about the missionaries when they are doing their work in the foreign country? How can we help them? First of all, we should look at the missionary and his work in perspective. Most have given up a great deal to go to a foreign country. They have given up all their family except those going with them, and all their friends. They've often given up nice homes and nice church buildings, nice cars and shopping centers. Would we do the same? Usually they have given up their own native language and must learn the language of a new country, a new world so to speak. They must leave behind many of their customs and learn the customs of the new country. Many even have a hard time obtaining food and water that are safe to consume. Some missionaries spend their entire years with digestive disturbances because of this, but are willing to stick it out for the sake of Christ Jesus and people's souls.

Most importantly, most missionaries do not consider any of these things as really sacrifices. For the joys and blessings of bringing Christ to these people far outweigh anything they may have given up. They have their difficulties in the new culture and have given up many material blessings left behind in our materialistic society. But as Paul said,

I consider everything a loss compared to the surpassing greatness of knowing Christ Jesus my Lord, for whose sake I have lost all things. I consider them rubbish, that I may gain Christ Philippians 3:8). The KJV refers to the rubbish as dung ~ manure.

We, too, can have the privilege of giving up some things for the sake of Christ and the lost, some of our material things. We can go with these missionaries in spirit and in other ways to these foreign countries.

Have you ever given up a certain pleasure for a certain length of time, and put the money for it in a jar every time you wanted that pleasure, such as a movie, bowling, ice cream, or whatever? If you've already cut down everywhere you can think of so you can help monetarily, but still wish you had more to give to the Lord through some missionary, have you ever skipped a meal and set that money aside? Paul said, *But whatever was to my profit I now consider loss for the sake of Christ* (Philippians 3:7).

Whenever we buy something new, do we consider it something lost by Christ? Whenever we eat more food than we need, do we consider it something lost by Christ? This is a very difficult thing to understand and do, especially living in the richest and most materialistic nation in the world. But Paul attained it, and must have enjoyed freedom from the slavery of materialism which no doubt was as prevalent in the days of the great Roman Empire as it is today.

Perhaps the best way to try this out is to be with others who want to give up something for Christ too. If it involves missing a meal, get together during mealtime and sing praises to God, pray for the cause for which you are sacrificing, and talk about that good work together. Keep before you the reason you are giving up your meal, the spiritual reason, and after it is all over you will feel you really did not sacrifice anything at all. You may not understand how this could be; but try it, and you will understand.

There are some who miss a meal once a month to help buy Bibles in the language of the people in a certain country. Certainly Eastern Europe, the former Soviet Union, China, and the Middle East are starving for these Bibles, with hundreds of thousands trying to get one for themselves now that they have been legalized.

Others miss a meal once a month to be able to send support to a missionary who might otherwise have to miss many meals without their help. Still others miss a meal once a month so they will have sufficient postage to mail relief clothing or food to a needy country. North Africa has been plagued with drought for the past few decades, and continually needs help.

Of course you should determine for yourself the number of times you miss your meal. It does not have to be once a month. It may be once a week or once every other week. You may do this until you have filled the need for which you were sacrificing - say, four months - or you may wish to continue indefinitely. If possible, do it with others. Your will power and the reason for your sacrifice may be stronger in your mind if you do, and you will be encouraging one another.

Sending "recycled" clothing is probably one of the easiest and yet most effective things you can do to show others how much God loves them through you. You can set aside the clothing your children outgrow, those you no longer wear for one reason or another, or something nice you have that you simply want to share with someone else.

Another source of clothing is a Goodwill store or any second-hand stores in your community. You could notify various clubs in your community who also may wish to help the needy in a particular country. You may wish to contact people on the last day of their garage sale to see if they'd like to donate the clothes not sold. And you may wish to set aside a place in the foyer or coat racks of your church building for people to bring their clothes.

Such clothing should not be fancy. It should not have any tears in it. If it does, mend them before you send them. All the zippers should be working, and there should be buttons on everything that requires them.

If the people to whom you are sending them are generally small in size, such as most Orientals, do not send large clothes. Save those for local benevolent work.

Also, do not send shoes. They are heavy, for one thing, and also most people can manage to obtain a pair of shoes where they live. Often the shoes of another country are made of different materials or are in a completely different style. Perhaps they wear sandals year round, or shoes made of rubber for rainy climate, or no shoes at all when it is hot. So save the shoes and purses for local needs.

Extra buttons, zippers, thread, and other mending supplies would be most helpful in keeping up the clothes. You may wish to donate used blankets or make quilts and send them along with the clothes. Often these same people who are poorly clothed and cold during the day, are poorly covered and cold during the night too. So do not overlook this need. They do not have to be a work of art and sewn by hand. Just sew them together on a sewing machine.

In wrapping your clothing and quilts for shipping, choose boxes that are not over a certain number of inches around, long, and wide. Check your post office for exact measurements for the country you will be shipping to. Apple boxes are usually a good size and thickness. They should not be over 22 pounds when packed, or whatever the present postal regulation is in your country. Tape securely closed. Do not be skimpy; these boxes will be literally thrown from vehicles to ships and back to vehicles all the way around the world to their destination. If there is printing all over your boxes, you ought to wrap them in butcher or freezer paper.

Then tie securely. If your twine is not very heavy and durable, wrap it around two or three times. Wrap the twine so there are four connecting points on each side of the box; that is, each side will look like a tic-tac-toe diagram. Then, using about four-inch pieces of twine, tie a knot at every intersecting point all over the box so the twine will not slip off. This sounds like a lot of work. But you want the clothing in your box to arrive securely, not hanging out, which does happen to boxes not wrapped sufficiently secure.

You will have a customs tag to attach to every box. In order to avoid custom taxes to the missionary or possible theft by handlers, on the side requesting that you itemize and give a dollar value for everything, write "Used clothing for relief - No cash value."

If you are sending several boxes, you may wish to write some code numbers on the lower left-hand corner of the front of each box. If you have ten boxes of clothing, on the first box write 1/10, the second 2/10, the third 3/10 and so on. This way the missionary will know whether all the boxes arrived. You may also wish to write the date of shipment below that, such as June 28.

Once they arrive at their destination, the missionary will go through the clothes and sort them by sizes. It may help if you write the sizes on those which are not marked directly on the item. Then the missionary will most likely take them to the family he or she knows of who is in need, tell them that Christians who love them are concerned for them and sent these clothes. They will probably tell them you are praying for them, so don't let them down with this. Then they will tell them of the God of love, whom we serve by helping others. Not everyone is converted as a result of being given clothing, but many will be, and all because you cared.

Another similar need that you may wish to help with is food. There is usually some country in the world going through a drought, or some natural disaster such as earthquake, or involved in a war. You need to write the missionary there and find out what would be practical to send. However, it is generally the rule to send foods that remain preserved for a long time and that do not weigh much. Some ideas are:

Dried Soup
Dried Milk
Rice
Noodles
Cereals
Flour
Tea
Salt
Dried Meats
Soap Powder
Bandages

Toilet Paper

Do not hesitate to send a large quantity of the same item. Variety is not necessarily the best policy here. Nutrition and distributing to as many people as possible to keep them alive is the main objective. Probably milk and rice are the most needed. The toiletries listed are also a big help.

The Bible is the foundation of Christianity. Clothing and food will help bring people to the Bible, but then they will need the Bible to go from there to become Christians. They need Bibles in their own language.

The best and most economical source of Bibles in the world is the Bible Society. The entire Bible can be purchased for around $5.00, and the New Testament alone for about half. You may write to them and request that Bibles be sent in the language of the people directly to any place in the world, and in your name. Give them the names and addresses of any individuals you would like to receive them. To obtain their address, call your local library information desk or look it up in your computer.

In addition to helping missionaries, you can be a foreign missionary without leaving home. World Bible School uses volunteers to handle correspondence courses of people all over the world. People all over the world register to learn the Bible from them.

All questions are multiple-choice except two or three at the end which are "discussion" questions which you respond to with a biblical concept. Your biggest challenge is in convincing your students to quit denominationalism and become simple New Testament Christians, thus requiring you to unteach some things.

You can grade their postal lessons from your kitchen table or internet lessons from your home computer.

A vital offshoot of World Bible School is World English Institute. Most of the people who register have never seen a Bible. They are the primarily the pagans of the world ~ Muslims, Buddhists, Hindus, Shamans or Communist atheists. Most are behind the "Bamboo Curtain" or the "Quran Curtain" ~ the unreachable.

Students with WEI sign up to learn English. Their textbook is the Bible. The WEI computer program grades the multiple-choice grammar lessons as well as the multiple-choice reading questions. At the end are two or three "thought" questions which requires you to correct the grammar in their sentences and make a simple biblical response.

Your biggest challenge will be to convince them to leave their pagan religion and believe the Bible instead of whatever holy book they follow. Often when people in these societies leave their religion, their lives and the lives of their family are in danger. Also, they are often isolated from other Christians, and you may be the only Christian they know.

WEI has certain criteria to qualify as a volunteer teacher. You will not have as many conversions with WEI as you would with WBS because many are not interested in or are too afraid to leave the religion they were raised in, which is often the religion required by their government. If they do leave, they often risk imprisonment and even execution, just like in the first century.

Your job is to plant the seed. Even though they may not respond to your teaching right away, some will later on, sometimes even after you have died. You must firmly believe God's Word will not return to him void (Isaiah 55:11) !

If you are comfortable teaching English as a second language, you could set up a language center in your church building using WEI materials, and advertise your English language classes in your local newspaper.

Whether you teach through WBS or WEI, you must never, ever forget what God promised: *So is my word that goes out from my mouth: It will not return to me empty, but will accomplish what I desire and achieve the purpose for which I sent it* (Isaiah 55:11).

If you do not feel comfortable being a correspondence course teacher, perhaps you can help with funds for advertising in the major newspapers and magazines in a particular city or country. Many countries have thousands of people who respond to such ads. These people are right now out there waiting for someone to reach out to them with God's word.

If you live near people who are newly arrived in your country and are just learning English, find Bibles written in both their native language and English. Hand those out to them, even if they are Muslim, Hindu, Buddhist. You never know which ones are dissatisfied with their religion and always wanted to know what was in the Bible. Now is their chance. Give them that chance.

Probably the average meal costs about the same as one Bible. Wouldn't it be wonderful if you could send one Bible a month to the foreign country you are interested in to help save souls there! If you have a family of four, that would be the equivalent of one Bible a week. My, the missionary work you could accomplish within a year!

If you have the Bibles sent to a missionary for distribution, you may request the missionary give your name and address to those to whom he gives the Bibles. Many of them probably will want to write you. And to think we take Bibles for granted.

Bible school material is very scarce in some countries overseas, especially if they have little or no access to a computer. There are few Bible school supply outlets in Europe, and probably next to none in parts of the Orient, South America, Middle East and Africa. You could gather pictures to send to missionaries and native Bible teachers. Your pictures should include outdoor scenes, food and animals primarily. The Caucasian race, which is the subject of most of our printed material in America, looks different from the majority of races in the world, and our buildings often look different too. Your pictures should make it easy for the children to identify with.

You could collect pictures from greeting cards, calendars, magazines (*National Geographic* is excellent), newspapers, store displays and Bible school materials no longer being used. If you do subscribe to a magazine dedicated primarily to African Americans, Orientals, or Spanish, you could send pictures from these magazines as long as they do not depict too much of the American culture in them. Colored paper could also be sent.

Send them "educational materials" rate if your country has that, and your postage will be cheaper than a letter.

Are there more congregations than preachers in some countries? Does your missionary friend try desperately to get around to as many of those as possible and then go to bed exhausted every Sunday night feeling guilty that he couldn't have gone to five more congregations that day? You could help with the preaching. You could purchase a battery-powered cassette and some blank tapes to send the missionary so he can tape lessons and sermons and have them passed around the congregations, just like the apostles' letters were passed around among the churches of the first century.

Do you have any CDs or tapes of hymn singing? You might write to those who made the CDs and tapes and ask if you could get a special discount to send them to missionaries and passed onto various congregations. Or you may know a group of singers who would like to send some tapes of their singing. These should not be used in lieu of their own singing, but could help teach them tunes of new hymns. They often receive words to hymns in their own language songbooks, but need someone there to teach them the tunes. You could help teach these people yourself. Worship is very important, and Christians all over the world want to worship; yes, they look forward to worshiping.

Don't forget the missionaries themselves. Send them tapes or letters occasionally. Or skype them. They are probably lonely and need someone to talk to, or to listen to, someone full of encouragement. Do explain to the missionary that their family does not have to reply to every one of your letters. For they are busy most of the time, and often very rushed ~ dawn to midnight. And how about sending them snapshots of yourself, or others of their friends or family?

Remember their birthdays! We all love birthdays. It is a celebration that we're here in this world, and everyone is happy because of it. Show them you are happy the world was blessed by them. Send them cards. Send them gifts. But be careful what you send them, so customs taxes do not cost more than the gift. Clothes and books are probably the most appropriate and appreciated. Or perhaps you could send a package of some food that is a special favorite and which they cannot buy where they now live. Plan far ahead of time for this and send your gifts two or three months early if they go by ship so they will arrive in time.

You could be a secretary to the missionary. If they don't use a computer, encourage them to dictate their correspondence and monthly reports onto a tape to send to you. You could type them up and make some acceptable arrangements for signatures. This would save hours that they could be using out working among the people.

Letter writing is a necessity to a missionary, for something congregations and individuals think that if the missionary does not write them regularly, they do not appreciate their support. Here they are out working their way into exhaustion trying to do the things they are supported to do, and do not really have much time to write. But they take the time - often around midnight or at daybreak, or perhaps during meals or riding in their vehicle. They do appreciate everyone's help and love to hear from everyone, and you could help them reply to these who are interested in their work.

Last, if you work for an international company, you may be sent abroad for a few days at a time or a year at a time. Even if there are only a few days, if you are there over the weekend, try to locate a congregation and attend on Sunday. There may or may not be a missionary there. You will come away from worshipping with them with a new and wonderful understanding of the universality of God's love. You may not understand their service, but during the singing, you will recognize many of the tunes. Just join in and sing in English as heartily as you would at home and as they are doing in their own language. God knew what he was doing when he insisted on singing in worship. It is the international language. It knows no barriers. The love flowing from your heart and that you receive from those around you will be just as dynamic as you ever experienced in the past and probably more.

If your company sends you abroad for a year, choose a congregation that needs your help the most and work with them. The members will have you into their homes and you will learn more about them there than in any international meetings at work or international courses at a university. They will reveal their heart and soul to you. They will laugh with you and celebrate life with you. You will also learn what their needs are. Jump in and help their congregation all you can, and when you return to America, tell the rest of us all about it.

Yes, you can do missionary work. There is so much you can do right from your home, or as a part of your employment. You can do all of this, and you can pray. Pray daily for the missionaries. And do not forget to pray for the people with whom they are working, that their faith may be solid. Your prayers are worth more than you ever dreamed. It will probably not be until we are in heaven that our Lord reveals to us how much our prayers did do for his cause on earth. Indeed, you CAN go into all the world and preach the gospel.

13 ~ SENIORS IN SERVICE

Is not wisdom found among the aged? Does not long life bring understanding (Job 12:12)? Gray hair is crown of splendor; it is attained by a righteous life (Psalm 16:31).

The influence of older men in the Bible is obvious ~ Noah, who preached to a scoffing audience (Genesis 6-7); Abraham, who grew old waiting for a son to born to him (Genesis 12, 15, 17, 21); Moses, who led stubborn former slaves for forty years in a wilderness (Exodus-Deuteronomy); Eli, who raised Samuel, the greatest judge of the Old Testament (I Samuel 1-3); Simeon, who recognized a special baby as the future Messiah, Savior of the world ~ Jesus (Luke 2:21-37).

How about women? Naomi, a near-ancestress of Jesus influenced her daughters-in-law, especially Ruth. Had it not been for her wise guidance of the young lady, Ruth might not have attracted the attention she did from Boaz who later became her husband (Ruth 1-4).

Anna, still living and serving in the temple in her eighties at the time Jesus was born. She immediately baby Jesus as the one destined to be the savior of the world (Luke 2:36-38).

Lois was grandmother of the early disciple, Timothy. Paul mentioned how he remembered that sincere faith which first lived in your grandmother. Paul believed that such faith "now lives in you" based on what he knew of Lois (2 Timothy 1:5).

Senior saints are very much needed. Those who don't get out much sometimes are just old in attitude, but not body. Perhaps they are sitting at home most of the time alone because they no longer feel needed. Their children are all grown, and perhaps they no longer have a companion. But Jesus said, "Go into all the world." He did not say when to stop. Sure it is hard and discouraging getting out and doing anything if one does not have transportation. But there are things the older Christians can still do.

Titus 2:2-7 explains, Teach the older men to be temperate worthy of respect, self-controlled, and sound in faith, in love and in endurance. Likewise, teach the older women to be reverent in the way they live, not to be slanderers or addicted to much wine, but to teach what is good. Then they can train the younger women to love their husbands and children, to be self-controlled and pure, to be busy at home, to be kind, and to be subject to their husbands, so that no one will malign the word of God. Similarly, encourage the young men to be self-controlled. In everything set them an example by doing what is good.

The first half of this chapter will offer suggestions on how to get seniors (men and women) to "rejoin the world." You can do this whether you are young or older. Next we will discuss what seniors can do for their special service.

You probably know some seniors who are sitting home right now doing nothing much more than being lonely and getting out of touch with the world. Try to get them out of themselves.

Call them and see if there is anything in town that you could pick up for them. Encourage them to call you when they need to go to the doctor or the drug store or grocery store. If they send out for everything and stay indoors all the time, make regular visits to see them for a while and get them started talking about themselves. Talk about their family, look at their photos, talk about the places they've lived, and things they've done.

If they live close enough, ask them if one of the children (yours?) can come over and see them sometimes after school. Or bring the children over to meet them. Most seniors can tell a story of "the old days" and fascinate children. If they play checkers or dominoes, this is a good game for you or the children either to play with them.

Next, try to get them out of their house, which is the second step in getting them out of themselves and into others. Seniors find it easier and easier to just stay home. There are actually some people who eventually have not stepped out of their own houses for literally years. If it is sunny but cold, ask them if they would please go with you in the car to have a cup of coffee and a donut at a nearby cafe because you don't like to go out alone. If it is sunny and warm, ask them to walk with you down the street to get an ice cream cone or something. If they decline, ask them if they would do it just once for you.

Then hopefully the next time the occasion arises, they will remember how enjoyable it was for them, and do it for themselves (and indirectly for you). If they cannot walk, help them into their wheelchair and go out on the lawn or porch to sit. If they don't have a wheelchair, try to get one for them. The March of Dimes is one possible source for a wheelchair.

If they have not been going to worship services, tell them you will pick them up every Sunday, and it will brighten your day to do so. Tell them you feel guilty going to worship with a half-empty car. If they are not too tired after services, invite them to eat with you in your home. Or perhaps invite them some other day of the week for lunch or an evening meal.

It seems that among seniors there is a stronger desire to maintain self-respect and dignity, perhaps because they know with their age they may not be able to do for themselves much longer. Therefore, seniors seem to want to pay for having things done for them. If this arises, here are some suggestions.

If you learn they can bake a special kind of bread, hint sometimes how much you love homemade bread. Or if they make woodworking items, tell them you need some of those things sometimes and would like to buy them from them from time to time. If they have a rock or stamp or some other kind of collection, ask if your child or you can come see it sometime and get some advice. They probably will not allow you to buy anything from them, but instead surprise you with a little gift, a little labor of love. Accept it graciously. Never deny them the privilege of giving. Enjoy it. And they'll feel blessed.

Now you are ready for the big step, that of getting that person to want to serve others. Try to get this person to go with you to visit another senior in town. Choose someone who will be enjoyable to visit. When you arrive, don't do all the talking.

Kind of moderate and keep them talking to each other with comments about, "Tell Mrs. Smith about such-and-such," especially if it is some place, event, or thing with which Mrs. Smith is familiar. This visit will then provide a possible friendship with another senior who has continued to be active and would be a good influence.

Try, if possible, to get your friend to come with you to Bible classes. Tell them how the younger ones would appreciate their sharing their experiences, wisdom and knowledge. If they will go with you just once, maybe they will want to return. If they don't have a Bible with large print, try to get one for them, or perhaps some non-prescription glasses from a variety or drug store that magnify print. Make sure they are able to sit by sufficient light to see and in a chair that is easy to sit down in and get out of and is soft.

Now to address the senior saints directly. There are so many things you are needed for. Perhaps when you were younger you felt you were too busy raising your children, going to jobs, etc. and never really got involved in active church work ~ Christian works. Okay, that was yesterday. Remember the phrase we often run in to now, "Today is the first day of the rest of your life." First indicates a beginning. We could change this a little to read, "Today is the beginning of the rest of your life," or "Today is the first day of your new Christian life."

Perhaps you used to try to do Christian works when younger, but for some reason were criticized or ran into some kind of trouble and got discouraged and finally gave up. This happens to everyone who works at some time or another. But you are not the same person you were then. Times change, and other people do too. You now have more experience in things to look for to serve your Lord through others. You are older and wiser now too.

Do not give up and say, I just can't do it anymore. You ~ all of us ~ have to stick it out to the very end of our lives. We cannot expect to work for the Master the first ten hours and then walk off the job and not be there for pay the twelfth hour. The hour of your reward is at hand. Don't lose it now. There is something you can do. Wouldn't it be wonderful for you to leave this world while doing some Christian work? What a welcomed sight God would be. Then you will be home for good. Then, and only then, will you be able to rest.

One of the last messages to Christians in the Bible is this: Blessed are the dead who die in the Lord from now on. "Yes," says the Spirit, "they will rest from their labor, for their deeds will follow them" (Revelation 14:13). Do not say there is nothing you can do, for there is something if you search for it. Remember, I can do everything through him who gives me strength (Philippians 4:13).

One thing that does not require a whole lot of physical effort is using pen and paper. By now you have read the chapter full of suggestions on letter writing and how you can do your Christian works through the mail. This alone could keep you busy full time. However, if you have arthritis in your hands and cannot use a typewriter or computer, you can use the telephone. Just refer to the chapter on that.

When you go to worship, are there moms or dads without spouses who have more than one child with them? This can be such a burden. Or perhaps there is a couple with many children trying to train their children to sit quietly during worship. Help out by inviting one or two of their older children to sit with you. This, in turn, will help parents keep away the temptation just to give up and quit. They will rise up and call you blessed time and again.

Something else you can do in a special way with your years of experience is to befriend someone in your congregation who attends services alone. If you are not presently aware of such a one, look around your congregation. You can bet that person either has no family or has family that is not Christian. Either way, they are fighting a hard battle alone.

They need help, for they are not receiving encouragement at home. If they cannot get family members to come to services, perhaps you can help by inviting them as an outsider. Often times a family member can get nowhere while an outsider can. Perhaps the teenage children dropped out. Have you ever had a similar experience? Have you ever known anyone who did? How did they handle it? Was it right or wrong? Did the children eventually come back? What influenced this?

Do you see how important your years of experience are? You have insight into and wisdom about things that young or middle-aged people may not have gained yet. Do not waste what you've learned through the years. Do not throw it down the drain. Pass it on.

Are there any fatherless or motherless children that you know of? (This includes absence of a parent by death or divorce or military service.) Do they have grandparents nearby? If not, why not become a grandparent to them? If they are young, perhaps they would like to watch cartoons with you on television. Perhaps you could read stories with them or sing with them or take walks with them or play games. Children love all these things. Doing them makes us feel youthful too.

If the children you have in mind are teenagers, provide someone for them to confide in. You probably will not have to discipline them, for they have that at home. But do guide them. If they do not like certain home rules, ask them what rules they would like to have. Perhaps they'll think of some that make as much or more sense; or perhaps after they've thought about it, they'll decide the old ones are the best after all. Do habits their parents have annoy them? Help them understand that their parents are human with feelings and needs too. Do they do things that annoy their parents? Help them think of alternatives.

Do any of these youngsters know how to cook? Boys and girls both like to create by cooking. Show them how to bake cookies in your kitchen. Or do they know anything about repairing a broken chair? Let them help you. How about gardening? Do they know anything about it? Let them have a small garden plot and plant their own garden and care for it. Often such things are left untaught. You have both the time and the knowledge. Use these things. Pass them on. Help them learn to create. Help them see how well they can do things.

After a few weeks or months with your newly acquired "grandchildren," don't be surprised if you get a phone call from their relatives or guardians thanking you and telling you how school grades have improved and there aren't as many school-ground fights anymore. And they'll probably tell you how their kids talk about you all the time.

Are there several children in your neighborhood? Sit out on your porch or lawn one day with a little plate of cookies or a liter of coke. Invite the first one you see to come have one or two cookies. Then tell them to go get their friends. After they've had their cookies, ask them if they'd ever heard about the boy who upset a spy ring (Paul's nephew, Acts 23:16-22), or the boy who fed 5,000 people with his little lunch (Matthew 14:16-21), or the slave girl who saved her master's life (2 Kings 5:1-23).

Once you have got their curiosity up, tell them to sit on the porch or lawn, and you'll tell them about it. You can show them your Bible and tell them it is found in there. Then you can proceed to tell the story from memory, and end up reading the last few verses of the story directly from the Bible.

Make it sound very mysterious at first, and keep them guessing by the tone in your voice. Then, as the story progresses, get all excited with them about what's going to happen next. Let your eyes sparkle. Smile broadly.

Then at the end of the story, find some way to apply it to their lives. For instance, you could say, "You can help grownups get well too by making them get well cards or stopping by a minute to see them," or "You can help Jesus feed people today by giving food to people in need," or "You can upset Satan's spy ring that goes around trying to get you and your friends to be bad by going to Bible classes and learning how to be good. "

Try not to make the story last more than around ten minutes, as children's attention spans are not long, especially while sitting still outdoors. Ask them if they'd like to come back tomorrow after school for some more cookies and another story. If they do come back, you have begun your very own personal Vacation Bible School ~ or actually After-School Bible School.

If they continue visiting with you, they probably will want to go to Bible study with you too, if their parents allow them to. They will do the asking. Then you can contact someone in your congregation for help with transportation if you cannot provide it.

Do you know people who are sick? Send them cards and phone them. If you can go see them, all the better. Being older, you probably had the same problem at some time or know someone who has and will be able to understand what they are going through better than younger people. Tell them you understand and remember what it was like. Of course, if you know someone who died of it, you do not have to bring that up. You are there to cheer them up, not depress them. Take them some flowers if you have a little garden, or a magazine, or some little thing you made if you like. Remember, every time you visit one of these who is sick (by phone or letter or in-person), you are doing it to Jesus

(Matthew 25).

If you know of anyone with a terminal illness, go see them or write to them. In this case, do try to get a ride to see them; for you, being closer to the end of your earthly life than most younger people, will understand things they are going through better. You can talk to them about how wonderful heaven will be. You can pray with them. You can give them courage. You can reassure them that God will be with them all the way.

Do you have any friends who are not getting out of their homes and out of themselves? Call them. Go see them if you can. Invite them to your house. Share with them of your new Christian experiences, and tell them how happy you are. Try to show them that this is the key to their happiness too. If you get your friends doing these things, that is a form of multiplying yourself, so you can be truly in a dozen places at once working through those you encourage and teach.

Yes, as years are added to each Christian, they by nature become wiser and more sensitive to the needs of others. And that includes you, dear senior saint. Because you are special!

14 ~ ASSISTED LIVING HOMES

"Do not cast me away when I am old; do not forsake me when my strength is gone" (Psalm 71:9). David said this to God, but often what he asked of God was what his fellow man had failed to do.

It seems a great number of people think there is not much use in helping the weak and sick and "senile old people", for they don't understand what is going on anyway. Well, let's talk about senility. It will help us know how to help "these people". We usually define *senility* as the traits of periodic forgetfulness and not quite understanding everything that goes on around the person. Consider for a moment what type of life usually precedes this "senility."

Do you recall the last time you were sick and had to stay in bed at least two days? You were alone most if not all the time and sleeping much of it. Recall, if you will, what it was like for you your first day out of bed after your illness. Remember? Your mind was working much more slowly than usual.

You were a little confused, for the world had gone on without you. (Even in a few short days things happen and change.) You really didn't have much to say. After breakfast, you went back to work or you began your daily routine. But you found yourself just sitting there wondering, "Now where was I? What was it that was so important that I just had to get done? Let me see, it seems I left that what-you-call-it over here somewhere." It was probably an hour or longer before you began to feel your old self again.

Now consider what it would be like if you didn't go back to your job and/or there were no other people left in your house ~ just you. What if there were no responsibilities for you to ease back in to? If there was no one around but you, there wouldn't be much housekeeping or cooking to go back to. So what do you do? You just sit. Perhaps you watch television, and that helps bring you back into the world to some degree, but it is very passive. The day ends, you haven't spoken to anyone, and you go back to bed. The next morning you don't get up quite as early as in previous weeks or months or years; for no one is expecting you anywhere, and you don't have anywhere you need to go or anything you need to do. So you sit again.

Then, after a few weeks, your grown son or daughter comes by on their way shopping. They ask you about something you discussed weeks ago. Your mind is rather slow now because it hasn't been getting much exercise, and your time orientation is a little off because of no particular experiences to mark your days. So you say you don't seem to remember that. They prod you a little and then you seem to remember and recall the events with them; but they patiently tell you that was another time. And so they go away thinking, "Poor thing, s/he is becoming senile."

Are you beginning to understand what senility can be? The result of not using the brain? The same thing would happen if anyone nearly quit using their arms or legs or any part of their body. Decrease of use creates weakness. The same is true with decreased use of the brain.

True, there are some seniors who are called senile because they are suspicious of everyone, or sit around and talk to someone who is not there, or who have to constantly wash their hands. Let's not give them that catch-all hopeless label called senility. If it isn't Alzheimer's Disease, let's call it what it is ~ paranoia, schizophrenia, neurosis. When we call someone "senile," what we really mean is "hopelessly incurable at this age."

True, the arteries harden and the blood supply does not get through as much as it used to. But hardening of the arteries has been discovered in young people too; yet we do not call them senile. If they begin to act unusual, we try to help them. Let us recognize these mental problems for what they are and get some professional help for them. Or if it is the dreaded Alzheimer's Disease, get some medications to help.

What about the some who feign deafness or bad eyesight or not being able to walk without someone right there? That's just a game. You'd be surprised how many of our older folks are playing this little game with us, and we are gullible enough to believe it! If they don't think they are getting enough attention, they will get a little extra this way. Society has been getting more attention with little games since the beginning, and this is one "sure thing" for older folks.

With so-called deafness we all have to take a little longer to say things, and pronounce our words slowly and loudly. They may even throw a "Wha-ja-say?" our way a couple times just to make a conversation take a little longer still. With poor eyesight, they'll need us quite often to show them where things are because, after all, they can't see. And anyone knows that if you can't walk well by yourself, you'll have to have someone by your side. See all the attention being derived this way? They know exactly what they're doing. It's a game. It works.

The things mentioned above are to aid you in helping seniors whether still struggling to live at home independently or now having to live in an assisted-living home. Most of what will be suggested can be applied to people struggling to remain at home. However, the major emphasis will be on seniors living in assisted-living homes.

They have much to live for, even though they may not know it. It is sometimes up to the outsider ~ you ~ to help them discover this. Here they are in a sort of hotel with no responsibilities, no purpose in life, and nothing to do unless they think of it. Remember, the best way to help people is to show them how to help themselves, and then how to help others. To feel needed and wanted is the foundation of mental well being.

There are various individual activities you could encourage people to get involved in to help pass their day productively. Many of these activities are the same as those discussed in the chapter on homemaking for others. they can knit, crochet, sew by hand or machine, encourage them to begin again doing these things. Ask the ladies of your congregation for help with yarn, fabric, thread, patterns, etc. If anyone has a sewing machine to donate or loan indefinitely, that would be a bonus. By all means, there would be nothing wrong with them selling some of the items they make to earn a little extra spending money.

They could help Bible class teachers by cutting out pictures, tracing things for overhead projectors, etc. They could help stuff envelopes for special church mailings. They could take a Bible Correspondence Course, and then become a teacher and help grade lessons for others taking the course.

These seniors are greatly needed by their families. Yes, we usually think of it the other way around, but this is not necessarily so. Their children out in the business world and raising children of their own are facing many things day by day. They need the encouragement of elderly parents, and letters from them would be appreciated. If they have arthritis in their hands and cannot write, perhaps you could let them dictate to you.

If they enjoy writing letters and notes and don't have arthritis in their hands, encourage them to get involved in activities suggested in the chapter on letter writing. The church may be able to donate paper, envelopes and stamps.

The men may be good at whittling and making little toys. Or they may know all about making fishing lures. They could sell some of them for a little extra money, or donate them to worthy causes.

Some of these seniors need to learn to enter society again. Their immediate society is the assisted-living home. Get acquainted with two people staying in the same room, if such is the arrangement of the home you visit. They may or may not ever have really conversed together before. Find out about each of them, and then kind of play mediator to get them talking ~ really communicating ~ with each other. You may have to ask one of them what they think of a certain thing, and then turn around and ask the other one what they think of the same thing. At first, they may only grunt a short answer. Be patient and stick it out. Show them you really do care, and others do too.

Go on then to another room. This probably will involve another visit to the home as these things take time. Do the same thing with these roommates until you have covered one wing or section, depending on the number of rooms in that wing. Find out about family, former occupations, whether or not they play checkers or dominoes, whether they sew, what part of the country they are from, and any other interests. You'll probably have to keep some notes to keep everyone straight until you get to know them better. But don't write them in front of the people; do it in your car or at home.

Next, pick out some of those with similar backgrounds or interests. Visit one of the more out-going ones and say something like, "Did you know Annie Cranston down the hall is from the same part of Missouri you are?" Or, "Did you know Charlie Brockwell down the hall claims to be a checkers champion?" The person you are talking to may not even look up when you say this, but keep your cheery disposition, and stick with it.

Then go on and say something like, "Let's walk down and see them," or "Let's invite them to play a game of checkers." They're likely to reply, "Well, I don't know." Encourage them, and unless they say absolutely no, help them walk down the hall or go get the person to come visit in this room.

Stay with them and try to get them talking together with leading questions like, "Tell Annie about what happened that time you rode a horse all the way to the county seat to get the doctor when you were ten." If their conversation remains a little awkward, stay with them; and after ten or fifteen minutes, offer to walk the other one back to their room. If they get a good conversation going on their own, then excuse yourself, and congratulate yourself for a job well done. After you have accomplished this, the main battle will have been won, for you will have got them to come out of themselves and "join the world" once again.

Lastly, try to get these seniors out of the home whenever possible. They are not there because they are terribly sick, but because they can't get around like they used to and can't keep up their own home anymore. Have you ever stared at four walls for months or years at a time? Don't let this happen to them if their only need is transportation and a companion to make sure they don't fall.

If it is a warm, sunny day, you may want to bring some friends with you, and take different residents for short walks or rides in their wheelchairs. Take them shopping monthly for incidentals. If it is cold or too hot, take them for a car ride. Take them to worship services with you on Sunday if possible. Have some of them into the homes of the Christians you know ~ beginning with yourself ~ for a meal occasionally, or even to stay overnight.

One thing that will indirectly help them socialize more is to encourage them to dress as well as possible. Some may not have any good clothes. See if you can get some used ones that are nice, some that a friend could make, or get a few dollars and take them shopping to pick out something brand new. Also, you may wish to obtain the assistance of some other ladies or teenage girls to come once a week to wash and set hair. When we look nice, we feel nice and act nice.

At this point, if you find that working with the people in an assisted-living home is rewarding to you and you would like to continue, tell the director this. Do keep in mind, however, that you are still a visitor, a guest. At any rate, you will be a sight for sore eyes, so to speak. Some assisted-living homes have activity directors now. If this one does, ask what you can do to help. If it does not, ask the director. Both will welcome your assistance, for they still rely on community groups and individuals to come in and help with activities. You may desire to continue helping only on an individual basis as discussed above. Or you may wish to go on to helping with occasional group activities. Here are some suggestions.

Singing is a popular activity with all ages. All too often a group comes into an assisted-living home, performs a few songs, and leaves. Performing is fine, but participation by all is more fun. Even a kitchen band could be organized. With something like this, plus a few songs the group knows well, the residents could have a performance in reverse. Instead of a group coming in to perform for them, they could send out invitations and have the people come to hear them perform. What a delight!

Probably some religious group comes on Sunday afternoons to hold a service. Sometimes one group does this, or it is rotated among various ones. If no one is doing this on a regular basis, be sure to talk with your elders about some young people coming out every Sunday for a worship service and visiting afterward.

In these services, do not neglect giving. This is as much a part of worship as singing. These oldsters do have a little money, and need the blessing of being able to give to their Lord. Do not deny them this privilege. Remember the widow and her mite? They may only put in a quarter a week, but it will still be giving. After a few dollars have been collected, tell them about some good works such as helping a missionary, a burned-out family, etc., so they may select one to help.

Something else that would probably go over is a Bible class, not necessarily on Sunday. It could be held for thirty or forty minutes since these seniors do tire easily. Mornings at 10:30 or afternoons around 3:30

are good times. Choose subjects that would be most interesting to them such as "Senior Citizens of the Bible," or "A Survey of the Whole Bible," or "Applied Christianity For the Shut In," or "Old Fashioned First-Century Christianity."

In your Applied Christianity lessons, you should include studies on being interested in each other's problems; providing someone to talk to; praying with each other; doing little things for each other; giving to each other; writing letters to people outside the home needing them.

Another activity for assisted-living homes would be working through the local library or community college to bring in travel films once a week, or science films that cover animals or events. More and more quality films are also being put out on events in the Bible, and they too would be appreciated.

Yes, there are so many, many things you can do for and with these seniors. Though it seems they are the most neglected people in the world, their capacity to love after a long and hard life is enormous. Let us not be guilty of so serious a neglect. Remember, we are to *Look after orphans and widows in their distress for this is religion that God our Father accepts as pure and faultless* (James 1:27).

You needn't ever think that going to an assisted-living home might distress you. Many of these seniors have lived there for years and it is their home. They love visits, and they long for an opportunity the "adopt" you into their family. You, in turn, can be an influence to show them the love which flows within the Family of God.

15 ~ NURSING HOMES

David lamented, *The length of our days is seventy years ~ or eighty, if we have the strength; yet their span is but trouble and sorrow, for they quickly pass, and we fly away* (Psalm 90:10).

It seems that life begins with such promise, and youth is spent in building dreams. Then the years progress and unexpected events change the dreams or even destroy them. Through strength of character is being built, people begin to think more of going on to heaven and leaving this world of cares behind.

The aged apostle Paul declared after a long and hard (though fulfilling) life, *I am already being poured out like a drink offering, and the time has come for my departure. I have fought the good fight, I have finished the race, I have kept the faith. Now there is in store for me the crown of righteousness, which the Lord, the righteous Judge, will award to me on that day* (2 Timothy 4:6-8a).

Those who have been privileged to live good and fulfilling lives look forward to going on to heaven. After all, that is our entire goal, and older people are conscious of being closer to grasping that goal more than anyone else. It is not a morbid thought to them, but a thought of delight.

The situation in nursing homes is different in several respects from that in assisted-living homes. Those in assisted-living homes are there because their arthritis is too bad, or they are afraid of falling, or they forget when to take their blood pressure medicine, etc. But all in all they are not sick other than the usual infirmities of bodies slowing down and becoming achy and inefficient.

Nursing homes are specifically for people needing round-the-clock nurses. Some people after a serious illness and returning home from the hospital try to get a full-time nurse to move in with them. But that is nearly impossible. So the only alternative is to move to a nursing home.

Most people entering nursing homes do not ever expect to get much better. A few expect to return home someday but most do not. They just hope for sustaining their present level of strength. Most expect to eventually die there ~ whether in a matter of months or perhaps years, but at least they will have friends around them when they do. Basically, nursing homes are extended-care hospitals.

Who do you see at nursing homes? Some are in bed all the time. Some are able to get up and be around in wheelchairs or walkers. A few can get around without help, but must hold on to the hall railings and walk very slowly.

They all nap during the day at various times. They have various forms of ailments: stokes, heart disorders, kidney or liver damage, cancer, advanced diabetes, advanced nervous system disorders, etc. They are not in need of a lot of special equipment which hospitals have; they just need professional nursing in sustaining themselves in their present state as long as possible.

If your desire is to help people in nursing homes, you will want to understand what is important to them at this time. Some of the things mentioned in the chapter on assisted-living homes would apply to these people, depending on how sick they are. Use your discretion. Working with people in nursing homes is different in that most of them are chair-ridden or bed-ridden. It is harder to cheer up someone who is in bed or sits all the time with drugs in their systems to help control pain.

However, you can encourage them to talk. Talk about their past, about their families, about things they are proud of having accomplished in this life. Talk about your philosophy of life and find out theirs. Read the Bible to them. Bring tape recordings of Bible reading. Sing to them. Find out what they would like to hear, and bring along a hymn book; they don't care if you haven't memorized the songs. And they don't care how beautiful your voice is, not any more than a child cares how its mother's is. The love is what is important. They can sit and listen to you sing for hours. Of course you can't do that, but you can leave them tapes or CDs of hymn singing.

Have individual Bible studies with one or more. Choose topics. Just because they are older doesn't mean they know all there is to know about the Bible. It may be all they know about is very slim. They may want to learn more now. Find out what topics they wish to look up, get yourself a concordance listing these topics, then look up all the scriptures you can find on the subject. If they don't have a preference at first, you choose one, and then they will as you progress.

Some topics of interest might be the life of Joseph, the life of Solomon, the life of Christ. Also the conversion to Christianity of Simon the Sorcerer, the Ethiopian treasurer, the future apostle Paul, the Roman centurion Cornelius, Lydia a businesswoman (ACTS 8-10, 16, 22). Also the books of Proverbs, what heaven looks like, who were Jesus' relatives, the mercies of God, forgiveness, courage, getting along, etc.

For those in both nursing homes and assisted-living homes, don't forget their birthdays. Bring a cake if they can have one, and baked with sugar substitute if possible. If they can't eat cake, bring a fancy gelatin mold and put candles on it. Have a little party, whether with two people or twenty people. Have relatives there or their friends or your friends. Sing. Take pictures. Bring along gifts. What can they use?

Skin softener, handkerchief, headscarf, lap robe, shawl, pajamas, wind chimes, picture, stationery with stamps, supplies for handwork, perfume or after-shave lotion, clothing, jewelry, jewelry box, a Bible in large print, a magnifying glass, a tape of gospel or secular songs, a tape or CD of the Bible, a game of checkers, a pen, a plant, hair oil, shampoo, artificial flowers, a colorful rug, a bedspread, nylons, socks, a large-print book, a magazine subscription, fancy clothes hangers, slippers, vase, picture frame, inexpensive camera, photo album, fancy cane handle, 100-piece puzzle, view master, harmonica, songbook, knitting needles and yarn, hand cream, comb and brush, shoeshine equipment, long-handled shoehorn, lap board or tray, personal papers box, boxes of greeting cards, reproductions of old family photos.

Worship services are very important to people in nursing homes. Try to arrange to have a group of young people (or any age) come and hold services for/with them. Not all will come, but a majority will. Even if they arebedridden 90% of the time, they will try to come. They will request that a nurse's aide put them in a wheelchair and roll them down the hall to the service. It needn't be long, but it should include all the "elements" of worship: singing, praying, giving, partaking of the communion, and listening to a short sermon. You may choose to sit next to someone with arthritic hands who cannot hold a songbook or a communion cup. Help them as the need arises, and reach over and hold their hand during the sermon or a prayer.   See Appendix B for my reflections of *They Worship In A Nursing Home.*

No matter what you do with people in nursing homes, probably the most important thing on their minds is dying. This is normal, considering their age and physical condition. You should let them talk about it if and whenever they wish. Often their own family may be so emotionally involved they cannot talk to them about it.

Help them with this. If you suspected you were going to die within the next six months or a year, wouldn't you want to talk to someone about it? Who wants to go through such an experience alone and without anyone to talk to about it? In order to help them during this time, let us consider what the older person's view of dying is.

Elderly people are usually not afraid of death. About the only source of anxiety is that they have never died before and it is a first-time experience. That is scary. However, all in all they look forward to it, for they are often lonely in this world. The family they grew up with and most of their old friends are now gone. They want to be with them again. This is an extremely strong feeling - an instinct perhaps - that younger people do not quite understand. As their body fails to function as it used to in youth, this desire grows also.

They read parts in the Bible describing heaven, or they recall them by memory. What are their thoughts of? They are of a great white throne with a crystal lake in front, and a ruby luster around it with a beautiful emerald rainbow above. They are of gates of pearl, foundations of a dozen precious stones, walls of diamond, streets of gold, and many mansions. They are of the tree of life growing on both sides of the river of life. They are of Jesus, the Way and Truth and Life. They are of living a glorious eternity with no pain, no tears, and no growing old (John 14:1, Revelation 4, 21, 22).

Indeed, their thoughts of death are not sad thoughts. The more we understand this, the more we will want to be with these people as they prepare for their journey to their permanent home. Their courage will give us courage.

Often they make up their own mind when it is time to die and rejoin family and friends who have left them behind. Examine any birth and death records, and you will see that deaths of older people who are relatively inactive come over half the time within thirty days of their birthday. Apparently they begin thinking about it and wondering what benefit there would be to live another year. Recall all the times you have heard someone say, "And s/he just turned 85 two weeks before," or "If s/he had only lived one more month, they would have been 90." Think about it.

You have heard many times how someone of any age was seriously ill, but just hung on and miraculously pulled through, for they had such a strong "will to live." You've also heard of someone who was ill, but not seriously so, and just gave up and died - such as a young person who had a limb severed and just couldn't face life that way. Will does play an important part in the final letting go or hanging on.

So often, one of the first symptoms of wanting to die and leave this earth is trying to communicate with someone close, usually a parent. They had relied on their parents when young children and weak in body; now they are weak in body again, and they want their parents to take care of them again. They may imagine they are out in the cornfield again, or are playing with their brothers and sisters, or are walking to town with their parents. They may even wander off from where they are living and re-enact these memories somewhere outside their home such as in the yard.

Please, if you are around someone while they are supposedly conversing with a person not really there, do not laugh at them and then shrug it off by claiming they don't know what you're saying anyway. They do know. Instead, ask them who they are talking to or who they are looking for. They probably will tell you it is a deceased relative. Then ask what they are talking about, and let them share it with you.

You may say kindly, "But you aren't really talking to them, are you? You just wish you could." They will most likely reply that they realize this. Then encourage them to tell you about things they remember about their life with these relatives. They so desperately want and need someone to talk to at this time and usually no one takes the time, no one cares.

The next symptom of deciding to die is that they will sit down in an old favorite chair or lie down in bed and just stay there for days and not talk. After that they will do what they can physically to carry out their dying, and begin to refuse food. This is the only way they can control their body to make it weaker on purpose. As long as a person is eating well, they are trying to live. When they quit eating, we can know they are probably preparing to die. Sometimes they are force-fed at this point.

(This, by no means, is an endorsement for euthanasia or suicide. There is a big difference. Euthanasia is giving them something to help the dying process come faster. Don't be a part of euthanasia.)

Be kind to these people during the times they are growing weaker and drifting off more. Encourage them to talk to you about it if possible. Sing to them if you like, and pray with them even if you think they are asleep. Tell them that, for the Christian, light is in the valley of the shadow of death (Matthew 4:16). Remind them that their guardian angel comes to get them (Luke 16:22, Hebrews 1:14), so they won't have to go alone.

{The author recalls Florence Cathcart at Harding University in the late 1950s. She had been in a coma, but suddenly woke up, stretched out her arms as though welcoming someone, and died. In the early 1960s during her last days, the author's aunt would stretch out her arms as though reaching for someone and keep asking, "Why are you hovering so far away?". In the late 1970s, the author's friend was reading alone in her living room, when her husband heard her say, "Hello there!" When he came to see who had arrived at their door, he saw that she had suddenly died.}

Your dying friend may still be able to hear you. Read the Bible aloud. Sometimes just sit and hold their hand or even lie on the bed with them and hold them.

It will give them comfort to know that someone will be going with them as far as they can in this world and sharing it with them as much as they can so they will not be completely alone for the "crossing over." With such help and encouragement from you, they might just possibly depart this life with a little smile on their lips.

16 ~ LOSS OF LOVED ONES

Job speaks for most of us when we consider death. *"Man born of woman is of few days and full of trouble. He springs up like a flower and withers away....At least there is hope for a tree: If it is cut down, it will sprout again, and its new shoots will not fail. Its roots may grow old in the ground and its stump die in the soil, yet at the scent of water it will bud and put forth shoots like a plant. But man dies and is laid low; he breathes his last and is no more....If a man dies, will he live again? All the days of my hard service I will wait for my renewal to come....You change his countenance and send him away"* (Job14:1,2,7-10,14,20).

What is it like to lose a loved one, whether by death or divorce? It is like an amputation. There is intense unbearable pain. There is mental anguish over the loss of a part of the person. The nerves still seem to extend into and out of that lost body part as though still there. There are the times of forgetfulness when the subconscious mind starts to refer to or use that part of them. That just insults the loss even more. The mental anguish cannot be described. A part of the person with the loss dies forever. There will never ever be any way to replace that lost part of the person. An artificial part or a part grafted on from someone else may be possible, but it can never and will never be that part which was lost. All there is left are memories.

What are the memories like? For those left behind because of death, the bad memories are sifted out and the good ones are left to grace the remaining years. For those left behind because of divorce, usually the good memories are sifted out and the bad memories remain. When loss is due to death, the question is, "Why did providence work in this way?". When loss is due to divorce, the question is, "What did I do wrong?".

When someone is left alone due to death, there is still insurance, furniture, and probably house and car left behind to help with their sustenance. When someone is left alone due to divorce, there is no insurance, numerous legal fees, and maybe part of the furniture and half a house and car if anything at all. With loss due to death there is dignity. With loss due to divorce there is shame.

All in all, the feelings of loss are very similar. There is much that you can do to help these people, for there are hundreds of such losses every day. What can you do?

You will receive a phone call about a loss probably from a relative, possibly a close friend. Go to the home of the family as soon as possible. The closer you are to that person, the sooner you should go. The time of day or night does not matter. The person suffering the loss is definitely not sleeping. What do you say when you arrive?

You do not say, "It was for the best; at least s/he won't have to suffer anymore now," or "Well, we all have to go sometime." Or in the case of divorce, you do not say, "S/He wasn't worth it anyway," or "Forget him; there's better fish in the sea," or "Now you've got all the freedom you've been wanting." The person may feel any one of these ways, but you do not know, and now is not the time to find out whether or not they agree. Don't take the chance of offending them or upsetting them even more. Just say, "I'm so very sorry." If they want to bring any of these responses up later, let them be the ones to do so, and then be supportive of them. They are the emotional leaders now. Be sensitive to them, listen to them, and sustain them.

Give them a hug. If they cling to you, keep hugging them as long as they like. Then they will invite you to sit down. Sit with them if you can, and hold their hand. If there is someone sitting next to them, kneel on the floor in front of them. If they do not wish to talk (remember, they are in the lead), just sit and mourn with them. After a few minutes, find a seat somewhere else in the room to allow others present an opportunity to continue reaching out to the person with the loss.

In case of a death, ask the family if they have contacted a minister yet. If they haven't, ask if they'd like you to. You can offer to call someone they know or your own minister. If they haven't contacted one by now, they will be happy to have your assistance with this. Discussions of the funeral will come up intermittently during the conversation. They will talk about it in general terms probably until the minister arrives. Intermittently as you converse, the new widow (or closest relative) will think of some other relative to call with the news. Then they will sit back down with you.

The general conversation of those present will fluctuate. Most people will follow the lead of the person closest to the one who died.

Their emotions will likely fluctuate. There will be talk of good times with the person, and talk of how they died, a little laughter, and tears. Laughter is used by authors of tragedy such as Shakespeare, and is called "comic relief," in order to release the tenseness of the moment. The human mind just cannot cope with intense irreversible tragedy without some kind of relief. Fainting is one way a mind short circuits. Laughter is still highly emotional and lets out some of the pent-up feelings. A little laughter sprinkled in the conversation of mourners is common and acceptable. At any rate, follow the conversation and emotions of the one(s) with the loss. Mourn with them, reminisce with them, laugh with them, cry with them.

The survivor may suddenly decide to do some housework or dishes or mow the lawn or something to try to get some sense of "normalcy" back into their lives. It is also a good way to release physical and emotional stress. Don't try to stop them. If they decide they need to pick out some clothes to bury the person in, ask them if they'd like to describe the outfit for you so you can go get them and set them aside until needed at the funeral home. Of course, if they insist on doing it themselves, abide by that.

There will be a few people who will refuse to admit their loved one died. This occurs usually where that person was young and died suddenly such as in an accident. They may go do that person's laundry and then iron their clothes so they'll have them when they get back home. Or they may fix their favorite food. Or they may get out some blankets to keep them warm out beside the road all alone. Do not jump in and tell them they're acting irrationally and have to face it. They are trying to keep that person alive in their minds as long as they can, living in their fleeting shadow before the sun disappears.

After a little while, you may say things like, "We all want to keep them alive just a little longer, don't we?" or "We wish we could keep that person here." or "We keep wanting them to come walking through that door, don't we?" They may not acknowledge what you are saying, but they will store it, and probably repeat those same words later.

By the next day, if the person is still denying it, start talking about the funeral. They will at first tell you there will be no funeral because the person is not dead. You may reply that there is going to be a funeral, and if the person is alive and well, s/he is going to be there. Or even if s/he is not alive and well, they'll still be there. So the survivor wouldn't want to pass up the opportunity to say goodbye. Also, other family members will be there, and they will need their encouragement.

Finally, if they are still denying it, tell them that everyone is angry because their loved one died. It is okay to be angry. It doesn't mean you are angry at the person, only the event. You can also start recalling with them past times in the life of the person who died. By referring to these good times and the fulfilling life they had, they will hear the person spoken of in the past tense, yet in a good way. And you can talk of heaven. You can tell about people living on, only in another world. You can tell them everyone may be able to all live together again someday in heaven. Usually by the second day, the person going through denial will begin at last to acknowledge it and being at last to cry.

This all leads to difficult questions. There are any number that will be asked during this mourning period, whether it be before the funeral or after. In Appendix C are some of them, with brief answers. Please turn over there now and read them. They are extremely important to this chapter and your understanding of it.

You may wish to bring a songbook and Bible with concordance and leave them in the car for use when details of the funeral are brought up. They will probably easily think of one favorite song but have difficulty remembering others. If that is the case, you may volunteer to go get your songbook and look up in the back where the songs are listed by subject and read other possible songs to them from that list. They may also mention a favorite Bible passage and may not know where it is located. You could help them find it with your concordance. Of course, if the minister is there, he can do all this. But you may wish to come prepared anyway.

They will need to decide what clothes to bury their loved one in. This is so difficult. Rather than go through their clothes, try to help them recall a favorite outfit of the person and go get it for them. Then place it behind a door or on a bed until needed. It will be several hours before the funeral home asks for the clothes.

During the two or three days before the funeral, make yourself available to the person. If there are a lot of relatives and close friends at their home, a phone call or brief visit would be sufficient. However, if there are not, you should try to be with the one with the loss as much as possible, taking breaks away from the home when other people come by. Part of that time you may ask them if they'd like to go to your home. You may offer to spend the first few nights with them, or invite them to spend the nights with you and go back over to their own home during the day. Whatever, make sure they do not spend the night alone until they feel ready to try it alone.

If there are many relatives from out of town and not enough bedrooms, you could offer your home. Also during this time of stress, and of making intricate arrangements for the funeral, the family is not much interested in grocery shopping and cooking. So bring in a few dishes to the family. Bring paper plates and cups so there will be fewer dishes to wash.

Bring by a large coffee maker or ice tea maker for family and friends stopping in. Wash dishes occasionally if needed. Perhaps stay around to be a "hostess" for people stopping in to offer their condolences. Answer their phone for them if it becomes extremely busy. Again, a lot depends on whether there is a large group or only a couple of people present. In some ways, more will need to be done if there are fewer supportive people.

There will be a need to take clothing to the funeral home, to select a casket, and pick out flowers. The close relative of the one who just died will have to leave home to make these arrangements for the most part. Be there. Provide transportation if necessary. There may or may not be someone around to help with this. If there are no relatives coming to help, you will be needed to help with this. Hold them close as they walk into the room full of caskets to make the inevitable selection.

The funeral director will ask for information for the death certificate which must be made out immediately ~ birth and death date, birth location, parents, occupation. There will be questions about paying for the funeral, questions involving insurance papers possibly stored in a bank safety deposit box, or veteran papers possibly stored in a box somewhere in the top of a closet. There may be benefits they do not realize they have. What about social security number and benefits? This will be a time of needing statistical data and yet the worst time in the world to force the mind to think on such things. The minister and funeral director will be patient and supportive, but a close friend or relative needs to be nearby also.

It might be a good idea to contact the family doctor if s/he does not already know. In some cases, stress becomes so great a close relative might not be able to attend the funeral without some kind of medication. Also a relative's own personal health may be in jeopardy at such a time, especially if there is a history of heart trouble, high blood pressure, etc.

By the second day there will be times when the family member(s) will want to go to the funeral home and view the body, possibly sitting in a room with it for a short or extended period of time. Be available to go along or meet them there if they prefer to be there alone. You may sit in another room to give them privacy, but still be available for someone to "lean on" also. At this difficult time, talk to them of heaven. Talk to them of the place with no pain or tears. Talk to them of seeing the person again someday. Talk to them of your own experiences. Give them a comforting poem. Quote a Bible verse to them. Tell them God will never leave them alone. Sit with them quietly while they weep. Sing to them softly of heaven.

On the day of the funeral, be prepared for a busy day, a stressful day, a day you can be supportive. Depending on how close you are to the family, how large the family is, how many friends the family has, you may wish to go back over to the home that morning. If there are plenty of relatives newly arrived, say hello, ask if there is anything you can do (they will know by now that you mean it), and then leave them alone.

If the family belongs to a church, someone from the church should contact them, offer the church facilities, and tell them they will have a meal prepared for the family after the funeral. Then, depending on how many intimate friends and relatives will be going to the meal, someone should contact other church members to bring food. This is common practice among churches, however should at least be mentioned here.

If the family does not belong to a church, do not hesitate to ask the day before the funeral if anything has been arranged for a meal to their knowledge. If they say that just they and a few relatives will get together in their home and nothing in particular has been planned, ask if you can help. If they say everything has been worked out, possibly in embarrassment, you could make up a couple of dishes to take by their home just after the funeral.

At that time look around. If the family is not noticing you very much, just leave your dishes, give them a hug and quietly slip out. On the other hand, if they begin introducing you around, it will be their way of saying, "Please stay after all." In that case, go in the kitchen, roll up your sleeves, and help get the meal together for them. Keep fresh drinks made. And as soon as everyone has eaten, clean up, gather up the dishes you brought by, hug them, tell them you'll call them later, and leave.

Make sure the close family member(s) is not left alone the night of the funeral. Then progress from there at the speed comfortable to the person. They may want to start spending the night alone right away or wait a couple weeks. After the funeral is usually the point of the Big Letdown. Everyone goes home. Do not leave the person alone completely. Yes, they need to ease back into the everyday life, but don't allow them to do it completely alone. Invite them to go shopping with you, to go get a hamburger together, to come to your home on holidays.

Anniversaries will be extremely difficult. The day after the death, the week after, the month after, and the yearly anniversary. Also anniversaries of the lost loved one's birth date and marriage are difficult. Often the first anniversary of the death is emotionally harder than when the death actually occurred. Sometimes people have their emotions under artificial control so they can think clearly to make important decisions as fast as they need to be made. Therefore, the pent-up emotions may not come out until the first anniversary, and at that time they may come out like the flood gates just were opened. You may be needed once again at that time.

Someone, perhaps you, should be sure to keep tabs on how the family left behind is getting along financially. If a woman is left behind, her income is likely to go far below that which was available to her with two incomes, and hers usually the lowest. This is sometimes a devastating blow. Now she must add to her burdens the question, "How will we survive?" Can she support the children if there are any? Will she be eating properly? Will all her utilities remain on? Will she be able to buy gas for her car and keep the insurance up? What will she have to go through to support herself? How many jobs will she have to hold down, and what types? Find out and help her work things out.

Was the one who died or left a parent of young children? They are as affected as anyone. Often they blame themselves for the parent's leaving. They have terrible fears whenever the surviving parent leaves, that they will die and never come back. Their fears are confusing and unceasing.

After the parent is gone, they will need someone to provide a substitute role model for that parent. Especially boys miss their father's role modeling, and girls their mother's role modeling. If you can help with this, invite them over to your home occasionally and do things with them. Let them know you are available to talk to any time they need you. Of course tell their remaining parent this so they can be aware of this help. They are very aware that children can go astray without a role model. Also, sometimes have the children over to your home just to give the parent a chance to be alone without all the burdens occasionally.

Along with all these things, pray for and with the person(s) with the loss. If you cannot pray aloud with them, then write a prayer and give or mail it to them. Pray for them when you are alone, and be sure to tell them you are. Tell them as often as they need to hear it. Before the funeral and after, perhaps for years to come. For the person with the loss of a loved one, whether by death or divorce, will feel the loss and pain for the rest of their lives. Yes, they will laugh again someday, and play again, and perhaps have another parent, mate, or child again someday. But the pain of the loss will never, ever, ever go away.

The day of a final divorce declaration will be different from a funeral. There will be no flowers, no soft reassuring music, no talk about a wonderful past life, no talk about seeing them again someday in love, and probably not any friends to gather with the person. This does not have to be. In fact, it should not be. In many cases the death of a marriage to a loved one is far worse than the death of a person through circumstances that could not be helped. Between the date of death and the funeral is usually about three days. Between the date of the divorce announcement and the day in court is usually about 300 days. There is still the crying, the legal difficulties, the confusion, the physical stress, the anguish. And added to all this is embarrassment and shame.

Go back and read all the above suggestions on how to help a person get through the loss of a loved one by death, and apply it to helping a person get through the loss of a loved one by divorce. Why not go to the person's home and comfort them on the court-hearing day? Why not bring them a little bouquet of flowers? Why not lend them a tape or CD of spiritual songs and Bible readings? Why not offer to spend the first few nights with them or let them come spend the night with you? Why not, the day of the court hearing, have a few supportive friends go with the person and then go back to a meal in their home? Why not share Bible verses, and weep with them, and talk to them about God's love which never ceases as well as the love of their friends?

Some people will say that they just cannot help people going through death or divorce because it is too painful for them. This is true for everyone. But can the family this is happening to say, "I just can't face it, so I won't"? Of course not. They have to muster up courage they never thought they had. They have no choice. And you can too. In fact, it could possibly help you face the loss of your loved ones someday. So often the things we tell other people, the advice we give them, are the same things we will need to hear ourselves in the same circumstances. So you will learn what to tell yourself when it happens to you. Try. Just try.

God will give you strength. God will help you know what to say. God will help you sense what you are needed for. God will bless your efforts. And probably at no other time of life can the love of God be poured out to such receiving hearts as now. They deserve to feel that undying love. And you deserve to show it to them, Christian friend.

17 ~ TELE-SERVING

Although the following passage from the Bible was meant in the sense of the beauty of the heavens declaring God, just perhaps we could give it a modern meaning. For, indeed, the waves of the heavens, the airwaves can declare God.

The heavens declare the glory of God; the skies proclaim the work of his hands. Day after day they pour forth speech; night after night they display knowledge. There is no speech or language where their voice is not heard. Their voice goes out into all the earth, their words to the ends of the world (Psalm 19:1-5).

Yes, God created all things to be used for his glory. Until only a few years ago, man could not imagine how the heavens and the sound waves within them could be used. But now we know. These sound waves can be captured by the telephone, the radio, television, the internet to "declare the glory of God." What an opportunity! For there is nowhere in all the world that these airwaves cannot go, and no language on earth that these airwaves cannot understand. What an opportunity!

Yes, you can use the telephone. The telephone can be your tool in serving Christ, and right there from your own easy chair. You could stay busy with this one work full time. And, it is not a variation of telemarketing. Let's see how.

Do you know anyone who is shut-in or sick? Telephone them daily to let them know you are thinking of them. If you know anyone who is blind, you could set aside some time every day to call them, just to talk or read to them. If you do not know anyone who is blind, your local library may. Especially for someone who has been shut-in for a long time and there is no end in sight, you could set aside a certain time each day to see if they are okay. This way, if they fall or something happens that they cannot get to the phone, you would know there was something wrong and call someone to go check on them in person.

Every Monday morning you could call your church to find out who was absent at worship services that Sunday, then give them a call. Tell them you missed them, and ask if there is anything you can do for them. Often someone was sick and wonders why no one ever came to see them even though they did not tell anyone.

Eventually you will find which ones are absent weeks at a time. There is something spiritually wrong with them if there is no physical problem. They have become discouraged or sidetracked somehow.

Perhaps they become Christians and no one followed up with them to teach them ways they could put their Christianity to work. New Christians want to work, and if they don't know what to do, they could fall away. Or perhaps there is a serious family problem and it is just too much trouble with too many arguments to bother going to worship anymore. Or a friend has been talking to them and has half convinced them it is not necessary to believe all the things in the Bible, and they don't have to "go to church" but can worship alone with nature. Or they have so many personal problems it is an added responsibility they just cannot handle, or they feel so dragged down they do not want to face other people. Or they are beset with a personal tragedy and break down in church too easily, so stay away to avoid embarrassment to everyone. Or they may have found something more interesting and exciting to do on Sundays.

They all need help. Often, however, they are too defensive to level with people in the church about what is going on in their life. However, the soft voice of a Christian lady can be about as disarming as that of a child's; only you have the wisdom to go with it.

Ask these people who have not been to worship for a while if there is anything you can do to help. Some at first will not trust your offer, or even believe you. Or they may think at this point that no one can help them. Be kind and patient with them. If you think you know what their problem is (it is doubtful they will tell you right at first), tell them what you went through similar to that one time and how discouraging it was to you. If they say this is not their problem, at least they will see you are sincerely interested in them, and understanding rather than judgmental. Perhaps they will then tell you what the real problem is.

If you feel you can help with regular phone calls to them to just talk things over, do this. Or you may invite them to come visit you in your home. Tell them you are interested in them because you love them. If you feel an elder or minister would be able to help in a special way and this person is open to the idea, ask them if they would like you to call them. Do get their permission, however, so they do not think you are gossiping about them. That would cut off all possible communication in the future. Above all, tell them you will pray for them every day. And perhaps you can even say a short prayer for them right there on the phone.

Does your congregation have a bus to pick up children? Often these children come sporadically because their parents do not go; and sometimes they forget it is Sunday, or just let it slide without getting up and getting dressed. You could offer to help by calling them and asking if they were planning to go tomorrow. This is an indirect reminder, and will help just in case the family is going on a trip so the driver will not stop by there.

Perhaps you can be at the parking lot on Sunday mornings when the bus arrives and greet them as they get off. And/or you could watch for them in the building. Maybe one or some of them would like to sit with you during worship. You could ask them if they had a good time and what they learned. They are likely to tell you, and be delighted you are so interested in them.

As you get to know the children better, when you call on Saturdays about the bus or car coming by and the parents answer the phone, you can say, "Did Johnny or Sally tell you about the scripture contest they had last Sunday?" Some children do not tell their parents about their experiences, and parents would appreciate knowing more about their child's activities.

If this child is a problem, do not pass any of this on to the parents. Tell the parent what the child did that was good and right. The parents will feel better about the child and perhaps their relationship will improve. Who knows but that you may be the only one in the world telling them something nice about their "problem child." This could be the beginning of a new life for the child and family.

Then you might tell the parents, "I'm looking forward to meeting you, and perhaps even seeing you there someday." They may reply, "Well, that isn't my religion," or "Sunday is my only day to work around the house," or "Sunday is the only chance I have to go boating," or "My parents used to force me to go when I was growing up and I just turned against it ~ but I want my kids to go." You don't need to reply to this except to add, "Well, you know you're welcome any time."

You may or may not want to invite the parents every time you call, depending on your relationship; however, it wouldn't hurt to invite them casually about once a month. "I'm still looking forward to meeting the parents of this fine boy (or girl) someday," or "Why don't you surprise me some Sunday?" or "We're going to have a special sermon on such-and-such tomorrow; I thought you'd be interested," or "We are going to have a potluck dinner right after worship," are some ways to bring it up occasionally.

You might eventually tell the parents on the phone that "there are some CDs that take you on a survey of the whole Bible, starting with Genesis, that you can see at home. They'd be fun and educational for the whole family. They are non-denominational and really interesting. Would you like to see them? Would this month be a good time or later after summer is over?" Of course there are other ways, but this is one suggestion.

You or a minister could follow up with this. For ordering such films, contact your nearest Christian university/college bookstore catalog. Your telephone conversation with these parents will cover months, or possibly years.

Have you been a Bible teacher in the past, but just can't get out as easily now? Or have you wanted to be a home Bible teacher and just don't have transportation to get to people's homes or they to yours? You may know individuals from down the street, across town, people who attend church and people who don't.

They may wish they knew more about a certain topic, and that topic lead to curiosity about others. Or they may wish they could just go all the way through the Bible and figure out what books are about what, and in what order the historical events occur, etc. Or they may want to know how certain people in the Bible handled wisely or unwisely certain problems in their lives. There are many possibilities and such people may wish there was some way they could get with another Christian to explore these things. The telephone may be the answer to you both.

How would you find out who wanted to study the Bible on the phone with you? You may hear a discussion in a Sunday Bible class and a person may not be completely satisfied that everything was covered on a particular question. Or a person might comment in class, "I sure wish I could figure out which came in what order in the Bible." Another source of people who might very well be interested in studying the Bible with you by phone are people who have just become Christians and want to know more as fast as possible. Some may not have transportation, or if they work out of the home, may want to just stay inside in the evenings and rest.

You may have a neighbor who you could just call and ask outright after a little small talk, "You know, I really get curious about things in the Bible and wish I had someone to look things up with. Do you ever feel that way?" (If yes, go on.) "It would be great if we could get together, but I just can't get out. What if we just called each other once or twice a week and looked things up while on the phone? Can't have coffee together that way, but we could both kick our shoes off and settle into a big chair and no one would be the wiser. What do you think? I've been really curious about places in the Bible that give medical advice, like keeping people with germs away from others. What do you think of that for starters, or do you have one you've been curious about a long time?"

If you have the resources, you could also use the telephone to glorify God by collecting some sermons, inspirational talks, and/or singing. Then publish the titles in the newspaper periodically, or list on grocery store bulletin boards, or photocopy and leave in doctors' offices and bus stations, or even mail to people. Or rather than collect tapes, you might want to use tape readings of the Bible. Or you may wish to contact "Bible Call", in Nashville, as they have been at this for over thirty years now and have helped others get started.

Another way you could use your telephone to serve others would be to work through a Bible class teacher who would like students to read some from the Bible every day. They could call you and read to you.

When deaths occur, someone needs to get on the phone and call relatives and friends. There is no time for the mail. People need to know when and where the funeral is, whether there is a funeral dinner, whether they are needed to help with the food, whether they are needed to sing in the service, and so on. And of course, after the funeral is all over and the family has gone back home and friends have disbursed, the close ones left behind such as parents, children, and mate need someone to talk to for a long time afterward ~ perhaps a year ~ as they go through the many phases of "letting go".

Other special events may come up suddenly and your congregation may need you to help spread the word to people as fast as possible.

Or if you have a small congregation and your minister is in and out with no secretary, you may provide a kind of answering service.

If you feel capable of it (as a friend, not a professional), you may wish to become a kind of "hotline" for people to call anonymously (you remain anonymous also) and talk over their problems. Or they may call just because they are lonely and need someone to talk to, even if it means talking about a recent television program, the latest news, a good joke, etc. Of course you can always tell them you'll say a prayer for them. You might even want to read a Bible verse to them pertaining to the conversation if they're talking over a problem. Remember, even if you don't know who you're talking to and may never hear from them again, Isaiah 55:10,11 remains true:

As the rain and the snow come down from heaven, and do not return to it without watering the earth and making it bud and flourish, so that it yields seed for the sower and bread for the eater, so is my word that goes out from my mouth: It will not return to me empty, but will accomplish what I desire and achieve the purpose for which I sent it.

You may be able to use the telephone to do some "marketing research" for the church. Choose at random 100 names and call them with the same questions, then tally them for a representative average of the community. Questions could include: Do you attend church? Where? How often? What should churches be doing that they aren't? Under what circumstance do you think people make a commitment to go to church every Sunday? What community need is the church not meeting? The results of your survey could be used to determine what types of advertising the church should do to attract people from the community. But keep it short.

A variation of the telephone is the citizen band (CB) radio and the ham radio. If you have a license, you can talk about anything you want to as long as it is moral. So you may wish to do some of the above this way, as long as it does not tie up the airwaves too long. Just remember, others can hear your conversation; there is no privacy. Of course, this lack of privacy could be more of a good thing than a bad thing.

Although people cannot talk back to you with this, you may have the talent and availability to start a 5- or 15-minute radio program. "The Christian Life," "How to Learn the Bible," or "Children's Bible Story Hour" are possibilities. A children's Bible quiz panel could be aired using local children. It could be just hymn singing. Contact some local stations and, if they are small and looking for programming, they may wish to use you. Or you may wish to arrange for it to be paid for and aired at a time of your choosing. You may wish to work with someone else to develop a call-in radio program for people to ask simple Bible questions.

If you have computer electronic mail and belong to a public bulletin board, you could offer a Bible correspondence course through your computer. Or you could mention it on any social media group you belong to. You can join a chat room where a particular religion is the topic.

Do you know World Bible School or World English Institute teachers who have converted someone from paganism to Christianity and the convert is isolated from other Christians (such as parts of the Orient and the Middle East)? You could sign up for Skype or other visual instant messaging service and become a Christian friend. You could even hold Christian worship with them through Skype. One major thing they are not sure how to do is to keep the Lord's Supper on Sundays. You could show them how and do it with them.

Actually, such visual instant messaging could be used with many of your telephone contacts explained above.

There are so many things you could do to the glory of God through the telephone. You can probably think of things not mentioned here. Perhaps the capabilities of the telephone are just being uncovered long with universal blessings. So, right now, as soon as you put the book down at the end of this chapter, pick up your telephone, dial a number, and reach out and touch someone.

18 ~ PRAYER PARTNER

No handbook on daily Christian works ~ Applied Christianity ~ would be complete without concentrating on the special work for which God has prepared certain special people ~ the bedfast. And of the bedfast, perhaps those of you who do not have the use of your hands but are paralyzed or disabled in some similar way, are the most prepared.

Why call it prepared? Because prayer takes time. First Thessalonians 5:17 says that we should give ourselves to prayer; pray without ceasing. You who are bedfast come closest to fulfilling this earnest admonition than anyone else in the world. You are needed so very much. You have that special gift of time with which God has blessed you.

Think of Anna who had spent probably 60 years in the temple devoting herself to fasting and prayer, both night and day (Luke 2:36,37). Certainly there is just as much need for prayer for the world today as there was then. Has God "called" you to devote yourself to prayer? Romans 8:28 declares, *And we know that in all things God works for the good of those who love him, who have been called according to his purpose.* Those of you who are physically disabled God has called for a specific purpose: That purpose is prayer.

Jesus said in Matthew 6:6, *"When you pray, go into your room, close the door and pray to your Father, who is unseen. Then your Father, who sees what is done in secret, will reward you."* Although Jesus was warning us not to pray to show off in front of others, he was also saying that we need to take the time to go into that inner room and close the door.

Perhaps some of us had a greater potential within ourselves of Christian fulfillment in the realm of prayer than any other work there was available to us. But we could not stop all our bustling around, and we could not go into that inner room and close our door. So God stopped the bustling for us, and God escorted us to that inner room and shut the door for us. Now with no physical activity we may do, we can concentrate on this gigantic need that we were too busy for before ~ prayer.

Walter Robinson once expressed it this way: *Private prayer is our refuge from troubles. High above the beating waves, and near heaven, it is our fortress. What sometimes would become of us, if we might not shut the door upon mankind, and find repose in our Father's bosom? The afflicted Christian, entering his citadel, says, like persecuted David, 'I give myself unto prayer.' You, who know all, and change never, are on my side. If I grieve any, I would not grieve you. I would not make you my enemy. I would retain your favor. Oh my Almighty Friend, say unto my soul, I am your salvation. Heavenly Father, your smile invigorates me. I am glad and safe when I hear your voice.*

James further encouraged, *Therefore confess your sin to each other and pray for each other so that you may be healed. The prayer of a righteous man is powerful and effective* (5:16).

Before sharing with you who you can minister unto with your prayers, think of all those people saying to you through the words of Alfred Lord Tennyson: *Pray for my soul. More things are wrought by prayer than this world dreams of. Wherefore, let your voice rise like a fountain for me night and day. For what are men better than sheep or goats that nourish a blind life within the brain, if knowing God, they lift not hands of prayer both for themselves and those who call them friend? For so the whole round earth is every way bound by gold chains about the feet of God.*

As you begin, send word to your brothers and sisters in your congregation that you wish to pray for them and those souls they are trying to help. Also, ask someone to write letters for you to any missionaries you know of in this regard. Then, as prayer requests come to you, have someone put up a list on a wall or anything else convenient for you to see. Your list will change as time goes by and as various answers come from God, so keep this in mind when having your list put up. Have plenty of room, for very quickly you will have hundreds of names ~ hundreds of souls saying, "Pray for me."

Do not get discouraged praying for anyone, for God works out these things just at the right time. It may take years praying for some ~ five, ten, twenty, forty. Can anyone afford to give up praying for someone during the time it takes? Whose soul is worth giving up on? Yes we ask, "Why does it take so long for some answers?" One answer is found in Daniel 10.

Daniel had just prophesied the coming of the Savior. Then trouble came up in the kingdom where he lived, Persia. Daniel prayed and fasted

21 days. On the 24th day Gabriel appeared to him and said, *"Since the first day...your words were heard."* He explained that Michael the angel, the chief prince, helped him fight the prince of the Persian kingdom and finally won on the 21st day.

Ephesians 6:12 further explains the princes or principalities: *For we wrestle not against flesh and blood, but against principalities, against powers, against the rulers of the darkness of this world, against spiritual wickedness in high places* (KJV). Hebrews 1:14 states, *Are not all angels ministering spirits sent to serve those who will inherit salvation?* And remember who Michael is. Jude 9 says he is the archangel, and Revelation 12:7 refers to Michael and his angels fighting against the dragon (Satan) and his angels (princes/demons).

To put all this together, we see that the princes (angels) Daniel told about were the angels ministering to the righteous as well as the angels (demons) helping the unrighteous. Apparently, while we are struggling against unrighteousness on earth, we have ministering angels who fight just as long as we do ~ no more and no less. And that, my dear fellow Christian, is why we need to keep praying and keep praying. God hears us on the first day. It isn't that he is trying to see how long we can hold out with our prayers for something. It is because our prayers are a source of strength to heavenly principalities. Apparently, as long as we pray, our ministering angels keep fighting evil until the answer can come.

God does not work in this world by suddenly changing events. Things have to take their natural course. People are not living in Wyoming one minute, and in Norway the next. It takes God time to rearrange people's lives so that all things are aimed in the same direction and come together at the same point in space and time to answer a single prayer.

Perhaps the person you are praying for will receive help in another city by a person who does not live there and indeed may not even be born yet and whose parents aren't even married yet. See how complicated things can get to answer your prayer? Our amazing God can work all these things out for millions of people all at the same time, and use his angels (our ministering servants) to carry it out. He can even keep all the prayers of all the millions of people sorted out and juggled and not bumping into each other so one doesn't interfere with the other. That's mind-boggling! Only God could do this! So, we need to keep praying until he gets things worked out and never give up.

The following comments are both for you who will be concentrating in prayer on various needs and works of the church, and for those who come to you for this help. Various Bible scriptures pertaining to those in need of prayer are cited to help you concentrate on the mind of God and God's ways in these matters. You probably know of others. Memorize them, or ask someone to read them on a tape recorder to be played to you before your prayers. These are not one-way conversations. God has things to tell you regarding various circumstances in life and they will help you know how to pray for them.

The first thing that comes to the minds of most people praying for the needs of others is for lost souls to be saved. Your prayer list will overflow with these people. You will not know most of them. But you can name them by name; God knows who they are.

Those who are trying to convert these people should watch for some physical problem to enter their lives and stand prepared for it. This is not always true, but in so many cases a physical problem is the only thing that will make some people stop and think about God and their spiritual problem, their eternal destiny. People may not start out very religious, but they still say in time of trouble, "God, why me? Why did you have to make this happen if you are so good like they say?" Now this is not a very righteous prayer, but it is a beginning of communication with God. And it is often God's way of shutting the door in their lives and forcing them to think about him. Their thoughts may not be very good thoughts about God, but they are at least thinking about him. Christians near to these people need to be nearby to explain this to them.

Fallen Christians are another subject of concern. They are often very difficult to work with due to resentments and apathy. They need your earnest prayers, for their state in judgment will be worse than those who never learned the truth (2 Peter 2:20-22). Often the fallen Christian will return to God in like circumstances as the non-Christian ~ grave illness, death in the family, material failure of some sort. Hebrews 12:5-11 helps us understand what is happening to them:

And you have forgotten the exhortation which is addressed to you as sons, "My sons, do not regard lightly the discipline of the Lord, nor faint when you are reproved by him; for those whom the Lord loves he disciplines, and he scourges every son whom he receives." It is for discipline that you endure; God deals with you as with sons; for what son is there whom his father does not discipline? But if you are without discipline, of which all have become partakers, then you are illegitimate children and not sons. Furthermore, we had earthly fathers to discipline us, and we respected them; shall we not much rather be subject to the Father of spirits and live? For they disciplined us for a short time as seemed best to them, but he disciplines us for our good, that we may share his holiness. All disciplines for the moment seem not to be joyful, but sorrowful; yet to those who have been trained by it, afterward it yields the peaceful fruit of righteousness.

Where do you get their names? Ask members of your congregation to give you the names of their immediate family members who are not faithful to the Lord. Limit it to parents, children, siblings.

Then there are those in trouble with the law ~ whether children or adults. Perhaps they have just been caught with drugs, or arrested for drunk driving or theft. Whatever their problem, it seems that most people in trouble either wake up to what they are doing to themselves and those around them when the first "awakening shock" comes; or else much later when they are at the bottom of the pit so to speak.

If a person turns from self-destructive actions right away, rejoice! If they do not, but get worse and worse, remember, those whom the Lord loves he disciplines (Hebrews 12:6a). Do not become discouraged and give up on them, for the Bible promises, *The Lord is not slow in keeping his promise, as some understand slowness. He is patient with you, not wanting anyone to perish, but everyone to come to repentance* (2 Peter 3:9).

Another obvious person we think of to pray for is the sick. You who are bedfast have first-hand knowledge and the deepest of understanding of the ill. You may feel a twinge of envy over someone who is not as sick as you and who will probably get well soon. But let us turn it around. The ill who know you realize you are physically worse than they. You can now give them the choice of thinking, "I sure am glad I'm not as bad off as s/he, for s/he is absolutely miserable." Or they can observe you and think, "S/he is physically worse off than I, but their spiritual health and strength are so far above mine, their disposition is so good despite their physical problems. If s/he can do it, so can I!"

Somewhat related to praying for the sick is praying for those who need to overcome personal problems. It may be that they have a drinking problem, or there was the death of a loved one they cannot accept, a heart-rending divorce, loss of a job, or some similar problem over which a person feels little or no control. Pray for them. They feel weak and unable to solve their problem. They are depressed because of their weakness. They've gotten so they don't care to even try anymore "because it won't do any good anyway."

For those who have a problem that cannot be changed, we need to remember 2 Corinthians 12:8-10: *Three times I pleaded with the Lord to take it away from me. But he said to me, "My grace is sufficient for you, for my power is made perfect in weakness." Therefore I will boast all the more gladly about my weaknesses, so that Christ's power may rest in me. That is why, for Christ's sake, I delight in weaknesses, in insults, in hardships, in persecutions, in difficulties. For when I am weak, then I am strong.*

It is only when we say, "Lord, I cannot go on like this. I cannot face life any longer. I am so tired. I cannot try any longer," that the Lord can step in and say, "I know, my child; so if you will let me live in you, we will walk together through the rest of your life and my strength will keep you going." Jesus said....

"Come to me, all you who are weary and burdened, and I will give you rest. Take my yoke upon you and learn from me, for I am gentle and humble in heart, and you will find rest for your souls. For my yoke is easy and my burden is light" (Matthew 11:28-30). When we cannot carry our load any longer, we willingly give it to Jesus who wanted it all along. In exchange he gives us his load, his work to do, and it is "easy" and "light".

For those who have a problem that can be changed but about which they say, "I've tried and tried, and I cannot overcome it, so why try anymore?" they need your prayers also. It is only when a person admits, "I can't," that s/he is willing to listen to God who can. *For nothing is impossible with God* (Luke 1:37). Philippians 4:13 reassures, *I can do everything through him who gives me strength.*

God loves that one with the personal problem, and probably much more than that person loves himself. They probably think that no one ~ even God ~ could love them like they are. But let us keep in mind Romans 8:31-39:

> *If God is for us, who can be against us? He who did not spare his own Son, but gave him up for us all - how will he not also, along with him, graciously give us all things? ...Who shall separate us from the love of Christ? Shall trouble or hardship or persecution or famine or nakedness or danger or sword? ...No, in all these things we are more than conquerors through him who loved us. For I am convinced that neither death nor life, neither angels nor demons, neither the present nor the future, nor any powers, neither height nor depth, nor anything else in all creation, will be able to separate us from the love of God that is in Christ Jesus our Lord.*

Yes, through their Lord, they can conquer. Jesus understands what they are going through. *For we do not have a high priest who is unable to sympathize with our weaknesses, but we have one who has been tempted in every way, just as we are ~ yet was without sin. Let us then approach the throne of grace with confidence, so that we may receive mercy and find grace to help us in our time of need* (Hebrews 4:15,16).

So do pray patiently and earnestly for those who have problems in their lives that they need to overcome. They are miserable, and they feel so little love. Pray that they will not be tempted beyond what they can endure, and will be able to see the way of escape, as God promised in 1 Corinthians 10:13.

Ask someone to read the newspaper to you each day, and pray for people who are mentioned in the stories ~ people who have been in auto accidents, politicians, people who have been arrested. Turn to the public announcement pages and pray for the newlyweds, new babies, and families in the obituaries.

Pray for members of the military put in harm's way. Pray for university students. Both groups mostly young people facing new challenges away from home. Ask members of your congregation to give you the names of their loved ones in these two institutions.

Does your congregation help support any missionaries? Pray for them. Most missionaries go to the field before they are old enough to be elders. Therefore, most of them are working without the presence, encouragement, and wisdom of older men ~ elders ~ and their wives.

Add to this the fact that they are in a country with different customs and usually different language, and the pressures can be great. They face either apathy or persecution. And there aren't very many there to encourage them.

It is very difficult to stand alone. But many men and women of faith did just that in the Old Testament days, *who through faith conquered kingdoms, administered justice, and gained what was promised; who shut the mouths of lions, quenched the fury of the flames, and escaped the edge of the sword; whose weakness was turned to strength* (Hebrews 11:33,34a).

If someone in your congregation is a teacher for World Bible School or World English Institute, ask for the names of their students so you can pray for them by name. If you also get the name of the country the students live in, this will help you identify them and concentrate on them better.

Pray for your persecuted brothers and sisters in the Middle East, Communist China and elsewhere in the world. Their identity is probably being withheld for their protection, but be assured that they exist, having defied their governments or predominant religion and became Christians. Daily they face discovery. Once discovered, they face loss of jobs, beatings by neighbors, their houses burned down by extremists, imprisonment and even execution. They are out there. Cover them protectively with your prayers. Never forget them.

Another group that faces persecution in these countries are those born Christians, but are always pushed to the bottom of society where they are only given the jobs no one else wants such as garbage collector, and not allowed a good education. They may have a church building, but periodically the building is burned by extremists of the local predominant religion or political entity. Sometimes they are lied about to authorities, and arrested and imprisoned for proselytizing. They can even be imprisoned and executed for giving someone a Bible. Pray for your brothers and sisters in these congregations facing these hardships for the sake of Jesus Christ.

Most people in such countries have never seen a Bible. Pray for people trying to get Bibles to them. Pray that the beneficiaries of these Bibles will be able to successfully hide theirs so they will not be discovered, even by relatives who would burn it.

Open your church membership directory. Pray for everyone in it, including the children. Remember weekly and monthly classes, clothing giveaways, food giveaways, business meetings, etc.

Give time to praying for your elders, deacons, preachers and teachers. The elders have such a tremendous responsibility as leaders of God's family on earth. They are responsible foreseeing that the word of God is not changed in any way, in word or deed, and that each Christian in their "flock" follow God's word so that their souls will be saved (Acts 20:28-31). They are responsible for the teachers, the work of the deacons, and the material needs of the congregation (Acts 6:1-4). They are called on by the sick for special prayer (James 5:14,15). They will be held responsible at Judgment for all souls under them (Hebrews 13:17).

Sometimes the pressures are monumental for church leaders, and indeed too much to bear alone without God. And knowing that all have sinned and come short of the glory of God (Romans 3:23), we should pray that they will grow stronger in Christ and never fall, as Paul warned that some would do (Acts 20:18-31).

Pray also for the leaders of the local, state and national governments around the world. I urge, then, first of all, that requests, prayers, intercession and thanksgiving be made for everyone - for kings and all those in authority, that we may live peaceful and quiet lives in all godliness and holiness (1 Timothy 2:1,2). Remember, this was written during the times of the tremendous persecution of the early Christians, around the time Nero burned Rome. No king or ruler is too bad to pray for.

Pray for your congregation as a whole that the Christians will get along with each other. Pride causes division. The apostle John said that *anyone who claims to be in the light but hates his brother is still in the darkness* (1 John 2:9).

No one intends to show pride and to hate a brother or sister. If you asked a person if they were showing hate or have pride, s/he would probably reply, "No, I am just trying to show the others how to do it best, and they are the ones who hate me. After all, I am concerned that as many souls be saved as possible." Another cause of unrealized hatred is resenting others in the congregation because they do not love enough, they do not show enough Christian concern, etc. The resenter in the process becomes the unloving person. Romans 12:9-18 explains proper brotherly love and ends with *If it is possible, as far as it depends on you, live at peace with everyone.*

Pray for people's enemies, and for God's enemies. You cannot pray for an enemy and continue to resent him or her. Jesus introduced this new principle in his famous Sermon on the Mount, Matthew 5:43-45.

You have heard that it was said, "Love your neighbor and hate your enemy." But I tell you: Love your enemies and pray for those who persecute you, that you may be sons of your Father in heaven. He causes his sun to rise on the evil and the good, and sends rain on the righteous and the unrighteous. If you do not pray for these enemies, who will? Not very many, I fear.

Last on your list is thanksgivings. Thank God for answering your prayers, for sending you his Son and salvation, for the church, for your family, for your material blessings, for his wonderful world with all its blessings, for modern medical knowledge. Just count your blessings one at a time and you will be amazed and humbled with gratitude.

Maintain a list of prayers answered. If you pray for all the types of people suggested in this chapter, you will average one answered prayer a day! That's between 300 and 400 answered prayers a year! And that will be only those answers you know about. You can double that amount if you take into consideration answers regarding people who do not know you are praying for them and do not know to tell you about the providential change in their circumstances.

If possible, send a note periodically to people you are praying for. Ask your congregation to help pay for postage. If you do not have anyone available who could write all these notes personally, you may wish to have some printed up, or even have some business-card-size cards printed up with a little message, "I cannot write, but I did want you to know that I can pray and I have been praying for you." Then give your name, address and phone number, and possibly a scripture such as *Pray continually* (1 Thessalonians 5:17). These people will be strengthened just by the knowledge that someone cares enough for them to spend time alone praying for them.

You may wish to get an attachment for your telephone so you can talk on a loudspeaker sitting on a table near you. Then, in this way, people can also call you and tell you how things are going. If your voice is strong enough, perhaps you could pray with that person right there on the phone.

Yes, you can spend hours and hours every day in prayer for God's work here on earth. In fact, you may wish to divide up your day and have a lost souls hour, a missionary hour, an enemies hour, and so on. Naturally, you will need to rest during the day also. But in between rest periods, you can work out a system to be sure to cover everyone possible during your day.

Prayer is powerful! God loves to answer prayer! The blessings you receive as a result will be overwhelming to you, to those around you, and to everyone for whom you pray. All those you know will say, *Who knows but that you have come...for such a time as this* (Esther 4:14b).

19 ~ HOME BIBLE STUDIES

In the course of doing your good works discussed in this book, you will open numerous doors to home Bible studies. Now wait before you panic. Through the years we have developed these terrible monster pictures in our minds of what home Bible studies are like. Let's see now. How does it go....

In order to get a study, I have to wear a helmet and shield to protect myself from the cutting remarks, tongue lashings, and stabbing replies. I'm just a poor lowly soldier of the cross and they think I'm their enemy. There's an army of them out there and I'm just one person. Even if I do happen to get a Bible study with one without being slaughtered, the slaughter is just postponed. I arrive, Bible in hand, and they greet me at the door leering. Of course I already knew before they answered the door that they hate me. They've already set the trap, and are ready to watch me fall into it. You see, they all have their little pet topics that no one can talk them out of. They immediately pounce on me with that, and I have no idea what they're talking about. At first we smile, but it never lasts long. We start slashing at each other with the sword of the Lord, end up enemies, and I leave. We may as well have declared ourselves enemies to start with like everyone else does and saved the torture and trouble.

Okay, let's start over. Let's get that monster out of our minds right now. It's terrible! In its place let us consider a quick remedy for that suspicion and fear. John explained it simply and to the point: "PERFECT LOVE DRIVES OUT FEAR" (1 John 4:18b). If you love them, you won't be afraid of them. The fear will be gone.

The first Christians certainly considered home Bible studies a pleasure, and you couldn't stop them. Acts 5:42 reports, *Day after day, in the temple courts and from house to house, they never stopped teaching and proclaiming the good news that Jesus is the Christ*. It seems this was a spontaneous thing with them. Let's see if such spontaneity will work with us.

You've selected some type of good work out of this book that appealed to you. You're giving it a try. You have shown God's love by letting your hands be God's hands. People have really responded to that love. Now they're curious about that love, that concern you have shown them which seems so uncommon in our fast-paced and suspicious world today. What makes you tick? They're beginning to want to be like you. They see a joy in you and an openness with you they want. So one day they will ask you a question. (If they've already asked and you missed it, don't worry; they'll ask again.)

The question will be either indirect or direct. "What makes you concern yourself with someone like me?" "You didn't even know me. That's God's love. How do you get that?" "Why has God blessed me with a friend like you?" If this is the type question they ask, simply reply with, "I'd really like to share with you my own search for that. I think I'd like to continue that search with you. Let's get together in a couple days." Their likely reply will be, "Would you really? I'd like that. Could my sister come too?"

The other type opening question will be like this. "I wonder what the Bible says about abortion." "What is heaven like?" "I wonder what God thinks about all this organized religion." "Why does God allow suffering?" Look there! They are asking you outright for a Bible study!

Your simple reply can be something like this: "You know, I often think about that too. I've looked it up some, but don't know if I've learned enough about it. Let's get together someday this week and look it up every place we can find it mentioned in the Bible." Again, their likely reply will be, "Oh, I've been looking for so long for someone to help me find out about that. I get different answers from everyone," or "Can I ask my next-door neighbor? We've been talking about it a lot lately."

Are you beginning to see the difference in this and the old stereotype? You're not doing battle with one another. For some reason we have this mindset that a Bible study means people are going to try to prove how wrong someone is. That's not it at all. You're studying to find out everything you have in common. That is a foundation for differences that will be discovered later, but isn't the entire structure. You will agree with each other probably 90% of the time, so need to establish this first.

After all, you are mutual friends mutually seeking God. This is why you do not have to be a Bible expert to study with someone. Learn together. In fact, if you consider yourself a pretty good expert in the Bible, try to back off and take a fresh look at everything you thought you knew. You haven't learned it all yet. Never reply with, "Oh, I know all about that. I'll come over and tell you where all the scriptures are on it." "Dear me, yes; I wrote my master's thesis on that very subject." "Our Sunday school class spent all last winter on that and must have made experts out of us all. I'll bring my Sunday school lesson sheets and I'll show you what we decided." Stay away from condescending comments like this.

Too much emphasis cannot be placed on your approach. No matter how much you may know on a subject, you must emphasize to your friend that this is a mutual searching as equals. With this atmosphere there will be no fear of one another. But before we go any further into what to do when you're studying with someone, let's explore some more possibilities for finding people to study with. They are everywhere.

Believe it or not, today's American society is more and more curious about the Bible. This is an educated society that wants to find out things for itself. And the Bible is up there just as high on the list as scientific discoveries, computers, nutrition, inter-relationships, world peace, the environment. Nearly everyone in our society will ask you a Bible question if you do a good work for them or bring up God's love to them. People overall are not hostile when they ask, especially people who do not attend church anywhere.

Many people have dropped out of their religion because of confusion. They felt as though they were just spinning their wheels and isolating themselves from other points of view, so decided to stand back and watch the religious world and the people in it. People are searching. Searching for just simple Christianity without all the formalism and national organization and titles and creed books. They want to know what's in the Bible itself. But as yet most believe they cannot understand it because they haven't been shown how to find things in it. Don't just stand there. Open the door for them they're knocking. Open it!

Besides finding these people through your daily good works, you can find them in other places. Do your neighbors ever get together? Do they even know each other's names? Get out there with some homemade jelly in your hand and meet them. It won't be long before someone starts talking about their problems - the perfect opportunity to bring up God. Tell them, "You know, I've been wondering about that type of problem too. How do you handle it?" Before you know it, you're going to decide to get your Bibles out and look it up.

Depending on whether you want to keep it one-on-one or expand it, you might say, "Do you think Chris across the street would like to get together with us? S/he was talking about that very thing the other day. Let's call." So it can expand until half the neighborhood is gathered around kitchen tables looking things up in the Bible.

Another source: People with special problems in common. Singles again. Ex-convicts. Wheel-chair-bound people. Military "widows." If you know of several people such as this, you might approach the most outgoing one and say something like, "I wish we could get together sometimes and talk about these things. I've been wondering what all the Bible says about this type problem. Have you?" Always find out if they share the curiosity before going on. If they don't, drop it and go to someone else. They're just not quite ready yet. If they say they are curious, add, "I really feel a need to learn more about this. I think it would really help me." Get another commitment from them. If they still agree, say, "Hey, let's get together over coffee and look it up in the Bible. Okay? And we can invite the others."

Or you could buy or make some invitations or note cards, and inside say that you're inviting all your friends with such-and-such in common for a little get-together with coffee and ice tea. Then you can look that problem up to see what everyone can find in the Bible that applies. Tell them you'll call them in a couple days so you can make enough donuts or whatever. The follow-up phone conversation should be friendly and casual. "Did you get my note? What do you think of the idea? Do you think we'd get anything out of it? Do you need a ride? I'm really looking forward to it. It's going to be just what the doctor ordered!"

Are there new Christians in your congregation? There's an old expression that we "convert 'em and forget 'em." How about meeting these new Christians whenever they make their commitment and say, "A friend and myself get together and look up different things in the Bible. Would you like to join us?" They are ripe for wanting to learn new things. They just learned an important new thing and that's what converted them. Now they want to know what other exciting things there are in the Bible just waiting to be discovered.

Or are you one of those who loves to meet strangers? You could find out who is new in your town or part of town and get acquainted with them. Tell them you have a friend they'd really like, and you are looking up things in the Bible together, and would they like to join you. This could build up to almost any size and be a form of Welcome Wagon through which to meet new friends.

Keep in the back of your mind your alternatives for when and where to meet. Don't wait until the opportunity arises. Probably your first suggestion should be for a one-time study only. Let's face it. As anxious as all these people are to learn, they sure don't want to get caught up in some "weird ideas" or arguments or a "trap" to get them to think some other person's way. You don't either. So make it casual and friendly and spontaneous.

Decide to get together to look up only one topic. Do your best to make it a topic that is easy for everyone to agree on. Even Jesus didn't bring up the meat of the Word until long after he'd fed people with milk. Show people with your one get-together that this is a warm, pleasant, reassuring experience. Discover God's love together. Then, after the first time, talk about how much you have enjoyed it, and the chances are very good they'll just naturally reply, "Let's get together and do it again." By going on a week-to-week basis instead of, "We're going to do this for three months," the spontaneity will be maintained without tension.

As to where to have your study, make it casual. The kitchen table is great, or a table in your workshop. At a park picnic table is another possibility. In the backyard on lawn chairs. At the coffee table in front of the fireplace. Sitting on the front steps.

How much time should you set aside? With this type of study, people are usually just getting into the subject after one hour. Two hours is a comfortable length of time and will go by fast. If there is the temptation to push it to three, try not to give in, despite how much you're learning. Otherwise you may get too worn out, not realize it until later, then hesitate to go back.

What method should you use to "teach"? None. You are going to learn together. All you will be is a "facilitator" to kind of keep things moving. You are going to discover together. You cannot say you know everything there is to know. Approaching your study this way, you will remain equals, and whenever an idea that is new to either of you comes up, neither will feel threatened. After all, you're discovering together. You're reaching for God together.

For your first Bible study, take only a Bible with a good concordance in it. If you don't have one, then get a small paperback concordance to take along. Don't show up looking like some kind of scholar. If you do not feel after an hour or two that you have found everything there is to know about your topic, bring more books next time, but not the first time. Do what you can as simply as possible the first time.

The discovery method is best to use for selecting a word that most represents the topic, such as heaven, death, joy, priests. Each of you should have a tablet of paper. Begin looking up from your concordance each scripture listed with your chosen topic. It doesn't matter if you've done this before; you can rediscover them. Both of you write down the scriptures, and next to it the basic point or points. Then go on to the next until you think you've found them all.

Then sit there and look through your notes, talk about them so you understand them the same (99% of the time you will). Then ask, "Well, what conclusion should we draw from this?" "So what point do you think God was trying to get across in all these verses?" "I wonder how we can apply all this the next time the problem comes up?" Then share personal experiences such as, "I wish I'd known this when...." or "The next time I'll understand what is happening...." or "This is really an encouragement to me. I'm so glad we found these scriptures."

When you are done, if you feel comfortable doing so, hold each other's hands, thank God for giving us his word as a daily guide in our lives, and thank him for your friend and friendship.

Will this method work? Won't people come to different conclusions? Nobody ever agrees. What am I to do if we don't come to the same conclusion? Don't believe that propaganda. Have faith in God's ability to explain things clearly, and your friend's ability to understand things logically. Believe it or not, 99% of the time you are going to agree! God would not be very smart if he gave us a Bible we could not understand, would he? Religious unity is easier than most people think if we'll just let the Bible do its work, simply and clearly.

Just remember to start out on easy topics (the milk) in order to show each other that it definitely is possible for people to agree on the Bible, and it is possible to remain friends, and it is possible to grow closer as a result. Then later when you hit on topics less easy to understand, you will have enough love for each other to overcome any fear of each other you might otherwise have had.

What should you do on those rare occasions when contradicting conclusions are drawn? Remember, this will seldom happen. But, when it does, remember that above all else, you are both searching for God's will with just as sincere a heart as anyone. Have this faith in each other. Then as you make the discovery that you are looking at things differently, you can say something like, "Perhaps we just haven't found enough scriptures on this to clarify it yet." or "I wonder if we're saying the same thing but just from different points of view." or "Maybe we're both looking at the same elephant, but emphasizing different parts of it." or "Well, I think we've gone about as far as we can on this for now; what do you want to bet it falls together for us later after we've learned some other things?"

Also keep in mind that some people are predisposed to understand some things quicker than others. Remember Peter not eating with Gentiles, and this after God told him personally that they were equal with the Jews? Or remember when Paul and Barnabas argued over who to take on a missionary journey and ended up going different ways with their own choices and both accomplishing much good in their own way? Remember when King Saul was ordered to slaughter all the enemy's flocks and he decided God didn't really mean it because they'd make good sacrifices?

Sometimes we are not ready or able to accept a truth yet. Believe in each other as you study together that eventually you will probably come to the same conclusion - a week later or twenty years later. Emphasizing our differences develops denominationalism. Let's emphasize what we have found in common and keep faith in each other and God's word to convict people of truth.

What Bible helps can you use after a couple times using just the Bible and a concordance? If you know the topic ahead of time, you can bring whatever is appropriate. Do not be the only one to bring these helps. They are probably in the public library, and would give others a chance to bring them too. Suggestions include an unabridged concordance, *Nave's Topical Bible*, Bibles of different translations, a Bible dictionary, an encyclopedia (for looking up histories of Bible cities, scientific discoveries, etc.) and maybe a small survey of the Bible. Stay away from commentaries. You want to create your own "commentary" through your studies.

As you progress in your study, watch closely for new comments from the other person as well as yourself. Comments each week to abide by the new-found truths is non-threatening if done by both and is essential to successful Bible study. God wants inside more than our minds; he wants in our hearts and lives also.

After your first few discussion times, you are likely to snowball in your ideas of what to look up (study) next. For in the process of looking up heaven, you may wonder about angels and babies. In the process of looking up marriage, you may wonder about abortion and celibacy. So keep a little pad handy for whenever you start to get off the subject. Stop yourself and say, "We'll never find out about this old subject if we get off on a new one; let's write it down and look it up next. What do you think?" Possibly for every session you will think of thee other topics to look up. Great!

However, if you are extremely self-controlled, you may not get off the subject. In that case, listed below are several topics you and your friends may be curious about:

So you see that you do not have to know a lot about things in the Bible to have a Bible study in your home. You can look things up together as mutual seekers after God's truths. And there are so many people out there looking for someone to do this with. Just remember, when they ask you an indirect or direct question about the Bible, they are asking you to search the scriptures with them. So why not smile and say, "Let's do it!"

20 ~ YOUR HEAVENLY REWARD

Ephesians 2:1-10 dynamically tells the state of our lives when we were unsaved and lived for this world, and how our whole life changed when we became Christians:

> As for you, you were dead in your transgressions and sins, in which you used to live when you followed the ways of this world and of the ruler of the kingdom of the air, the spirit who is now at work in those who are disobedient. All of us also lived among them at one time, gratifying the cravings of our sinful nature and following his desires and thoughts. Like the rest, we were by nature objects of wrath.

> *But because of his great love for us, God, who is rich in mercy, made us alive with Christ even when we were dead in transgressions - it is by grace you have been saved. And God raised us up with Christ and seated us with him in the heavenly realms in Christ Jesus, in order that in the coming ages he might show the incomparable riches of his grace, expressed in his kindness to us in Christ Jesus.*

> *For it is by grace you have been saved; through faith - and this not from yourselves, it is the gifts of God -not by works, so that no one can boast. For we are GOD'S WORKMANSHIP, CREATED IN CHRIST JESUS TO DO GOOD WORKS, WHICH GOD PREPARED IN ADVANCE FOR US TO DO.*

Yes, we should never boast of our good works, for that is what we were created for. We were depraved sinners, doing things for our own selfish interests and desires only, not deserving the God we sinned against. But he loved us, his enemies, and sacrificed his most precious possession ~ his only Son ~ so we could live with him eternally. This was God's free gift to us. We did nothing to deserve it or pay for it, nor can we ever.

God, then, made a way for us to be created again, born again in Christ Jesus. Jesus took the punishment for our sins in his death, then was buried and raised unto a new life as Savior of the world. So if we have faith in what Jesus did, we can follow his example in a spiritual way by dying spiritually, being buried in water symbolically, and being raised a new spiritual being. Look at Romans 6:1-13:

Or don't you know that all of us who were baptized into Christ Jesus were baptized into his death? We were therefore buried with him through baptism into death in order that, just as Christ was raised from the dead through the glory of the Father, we too may live a new life.

If we have been united with him in his death, we will certainly also be united with him in his resurrection. For we know that our old self was crucified with him so that the body of sin might be rendered powerless, that we should no longer be slaves to sin ~ because anyone who has died has been freed from sin.

Now, if we died with Christ, we believe that we will also live with him. For we know that since Christ was raised from the dead, he cannot die again; death no longer has mastery over him. The death he died, he died to sin once for all; but the life he lives, he lives to God.

In the same way, count yourselves dead to sin but alive to God in Christ Jesus. Therefore do not let sin reign in your mortal body so that you obey its evil desires. Do not offer the parts of your body to sin, as instruments of wickedness, but rather offer yourselves to God, as those who have been brought from death to life; and offer the parts of your body to him as instruments of righteousness.

Yes, the members of our body no longer belong to ourselves to use for selfish purposes. The members of our body ~ our hands, our feet, our voice, our mind ~ are now instruments of righteousness to God. If our members have not become God's, then when we were baptized we were merely buried in water, but nothing spiritual happened. We did not rise up to a resurrected new life as Jesus did. Naturally, the babe in Christ does not understand this completely, but is expected to be continually learning more of it and practicing more and more of it all the time.

Did you catch what was said in Ephesians above that Jesus does to us when we are made alive together in him? He raises us up with him, and seats us with him on his throne in the heavenly places! Remember, the greatest in the kingdom is servant of all (Mark 10:43-45). And as servants, Jesus Christ has *loved us, and washed us from our sins in his blood, and has made us kings and priests unto God and his Father* (Revelation 1:5b-6a, KJV).

1 Peter 2:5,9 explains further the holy priesthood: *You also, like living stones, are being built into a spiritual house to be a holy priesthood,*

offering spiritual sacrifices acceptable to God through Jesus Christ. But you are a chosen people, a royal priesthood, a holy nation, a people belonging to God, that you may declare the praises of him who called you out of darkness into his wonderful light.

Yes, as living stones we are built up into a spiritual house, the temple of God, which are our bodies. *Don't you know that you yourselves are God's temple and that God's Spirit lives in you?* (1 Corinthians 3:16). Our bodies are living stones created into living temples to God. We are at the same time the royal priests in these living temples. *Therefore, I urge you, brothers, in view of God's mercy, to offer your bodies as living sacrifices, holy and pleasing to God - which is your spiritual worship* (Romans 12:1).

As spiritual kings and priests, reigning over our bodies that are now dedicated to the heavenly and not the earthly, we have crowns. Over and over in Revelation chapters 2 and 3 Jesus sends his message to the churches and says, *"I know your deeds."* Then in chapter 3, verse 11, our Savior admonishes, *"I am coming soon. Hold on to what you have, so that no one will take your crown."*

Indeed, there will always be those who will try to discourage you from doing your good deeds and take your crown away, whether they be the ungrateful, the critical, the overly dependent, family, friends, weaker Christian brothers and sisters. Do not let anyone ever take your crown away from you.

Do not suppose that I have come to bring peace to the earth. I did not come to bring peace, but a sword. For I have come to turn a man against his father, a daughter against her mother, a daughter-in-law against her mother-in-law ~ man's enemies will be the members of his own household. Anyone who loves his father or mother more than me is not worthy of me; anyone who loves his son or daughter more than me is not worthy of me; and anyone who does not take his cross and follow me is not worthy of me. Whoever finds his life will lose it, and whoever loses his life will find it. He who receives you receives me, and he who receives me receives the one who sent me (Matthew 10:34-40).

In a worldly sense, you will have less peace, for you will always be concerned about the troubles and needs of others. You would have greater peace if you just went your way and pretended those people did not exist. However, in the long run, that is not peace; for the world continues to suffer, and you have not spread love (God) throughout the world. Jesus said, "*I have told you these things, so that in me you may have peace. In this world you will have trouble. But take heart! I have overcome the world*" (John 16:33).

Yes, if you go around helping others and trying to bring peace among people who are not at peace with each other, and trying to bring peace between mankind and God, you will be hated by worldly people who do not want to get along with each other, and who do not care to get along with God. But remember Jesus' words of reassurance, "Blessed are the peacemakers, for they will be called sons of God" (Matthew 5:9).

Therefore, my dear brothers, stand firm. Let nothing move you. Always give yourselves fully to the work of the Lord, because you know that your labor in the Lord is not in vain (1 Corinthians 15:58). There will be some people you will try to help who will not want your help, or who will twist around your motives. Or you will sometimes become so tired because there seems to be so much to do. The more work you do, the more work you will see that needs to be done. You will become exhausted sometimes to the point of giving it all up. Moses went through this himself. In Numbers 11:10-15, he cried to his God in sheer exhaustion at trying to lead and help some three million people all by himself:

Moses heard the people of every family wailing, each at the entrance to his tent. The Lord became exceedingly angry, and Moses was troubled. He asked the Lord, "Why have you brought this trouble on your servant? What have I done to displease you that you put the burden of all these people on me? Did I conceive all these people? Did I give them birth? Why do you tell me to carry them in my arms, as a nurse carries an infant, to the land you promised on oath to their forefathers? Where can I get meat for all these people? They keep wailing to me, 'Give us meat to eat!' I cannot carry all these people by myself; the burden is too heavy for me. If this is how you are going to treat me, put me to death right now ~ if I have found favor in your eyes ~ and do not let me face my own ruin."

There for awhile Moses began thinking something many people find themselves thinking once they have gotten deeply involved in helping with the spiritual and physical needs of the world. He thought he had to do it all by himself, and he was buckling under the load.

Moses was wrong. God told him to find seventy others to help him. Moses had to multiply himself by training others. When you begin to feel such a strain, multiply yourself. Find others to take with you and train, so they can take their rightful place beside you. As you do your part, know that God will do his part. Remember, we are workers together with God (2 Corinthians 6:1), and with God nothing is impossible (Matthew 19:26).

Paul, who was beaten down so many times during his ministry, and each time got back up, reassures us in 1 Corinthians 15:57,58: *But thanks be to God! He gives us the victory through our Lord Jesus Christ. Therefore, my dear brothers, stand firm. Let nothing move you. Always give yourselves fully to the work of the Lord, because you know that your labor in the Lord is not in vain.*

We are further encouraged by Galatians 6:9, which declares, *Let us not become weary in doing good, for at the proper time we will reap a harvest if we do not give up.* In that last day when our eternal destination is pronounced, we can depend on the righteous judgment of God who *will give to each person according to what he has done. To those who by persistence in doing good seek glory, honor and immortality, he will give eternal life* (Romans 2:6,7).

God is not unjust; he will not forget your work and the love you have shown him as you have helped his people and continue to help them. We want each of you to show this same diligence to the very end, in order to make your hope sure. We do not want you to become lazy, but to imitate those who through faith and patience inherit what has been promised (Hebrews 6:10-12).

In the evening when you have worked all day for your Lord, and you are tired and wonder if you can stick it out another ten years or even fifty years, think on Revelation 14:13: *Then I heard a voice from heaven say, "Write: Blessed are the dead who die in the Lord from now on." "Yes," says the Spirit, "they will rest from their labor, for their deeds will follow them."*

We will have no real rest until we arrive at our destination with all the other souls we have influenced and taught there with us. After all, compared with eternity, *what is your life? You are a mist that appears for a little while and then vanishes from this earth* (James 4:14).

At the end of your life, you will be able to say confidently with Paul the great tireless apostle, "*I have fought the good fight, I have finished the race, I have kept the faith. Now there is in store for me the crown of righteousness, which the Lord the righteous Judge, will award to me on that day*

~ and not only to me, but also to all who have longed for his appearing" (2 Timothy 4:7,8).

Just what will be our reward? We know that heaven will be a place prepared for us (1 Corinthians 2:9; John 14:3). We also know that God hates idleness and considers it one of the prime sins of Sodom (Ezekiel 16:49). Therefore, there could not be idleness in heaven. There will be much worshipping, much singing (Revelation 19:1-6). Perhaps, too, there is an indication that in heaven we will have a greater job to do than we have ever had on earth; perhaps this is why our earthly journey is considered a testing ground, and is so vitally important.

Matthew 25 describes the kingdom of heaven and the judgment day. Those who used their God-given talents and multiplied them for their Lord through constant use were told, *"Well done, good and faithful servant! You have been faithful with a few things; I will put you in charge of many things. Come and share your master's happiness"* (verse 21, 23). Similarly, Luke tells us about a king who went away and left his servants in charge of certain things with a certain amount of money. When he returned he said, *"Well done, my good servant! Because you have been trustworthy in a very small matter, take charge of ten cities"* (Luke 19:17).

Just what has God been preparing us for? Just what does he have in mind for the characteristics he is developing in us on earth in the midst of people pressuring us to give in? What tasks, what cities, what glories? We don't know. All we do know is we will never get tired.

If we continue to work, the time will pass before we know it, and Jesus' last message of love to us will be fulfilled at last: *"Behold, I am coming soon! My reward is with me, and I will give to everyone according to what he has done. I am the Alpha and the Omega, the First and the Last, the Beginning and the End....Yes, I am coming soon"* (Revelation 22:12,13,20b).

Let us add in resounding unison, *"Amen! Come, Lord Jesus!"*

Appendix A
175 GOOD WORKS FOR
BIBLE SCHOOL CLASSES

1. ADAM AND EVE: Plant some house plants to be given to newcomers to the community or church, or to convalescents.

2. CAIN AND ABEL: Write letters to be sent to a prison or juvenile home.

3. TOWER OF BABEL: Make invitations for your friends to come to Bible study so they can reach God through the tower of scriptures.

4. NOAH AND THE ARK: Go out on the lawn and throw bread crumbs to the birds.

5. ABRAHAM AND SARAH MOVE: Make "Welcome to Our Town" cards to give newcomers.

6. ABRAHAM AND LOT DIVIDE THEIR LAND: Bring an item of clothing that is good to give away.

7. ABRAHAM AND SARAH HAVE A SON: Make and send cards to one or more parents in the newspaper who just had a baby.

8 LOT/SODOM AND GOMORRAH: Bring some money to buy Bibles to give visitors or people in other nations.

9. HAGAR AND ISHMAEL WANDER: Bring some food to give to someone in need.

10. ABRAHAM OFFERS ISAAC: Sacrifice some clothing and bring it to give someone in need.

11. ISAAC MARRIES REBECCA: Have a special prayer for everyone in your class for their future husband or wife, whoever or wherever they may be.

12. ESAU SELLS HIS BIRTHRIGHT TO JACOB: Make scrapbooks of God's gifts to his children to send children in the hospital.

13. JACOB DECEIVES ISAAC: Buy a Braille Bible for a blind person, or make a Braille greeting card.

14. JACOB AND THE ANGELS ON THE LADDER: Make cards about heaven to send nursing home patients.

15. JACOB WORKS 14 YEARS FOR RACHAEL: Write a Christian or neighbor asking if you may do odd jobs all week to pay for postage to send clothing to a missionary.

16. JOSEPH SOLD BY JEALOUS BROTHERS: Send a card to a friend who recently won something and tell them you are glad.

17. JOSEPH INTERPRETS DREAMS IN JAIL: Send a letter or card

to a prisoner or someone you may know who just got out of jail.

18. THE SEVEN-YEAR FAMINE IN EGYPT: Bring food to give someone in need.

19. JOSEPH FORGIVES HIS BROTHERS: Write a letter or card to someone you treated badly this week and tell them you're sorry.

20. MOSES FOUND BY PHAROAH'S DAUGHTER: Send cards to someone with a new baby.

21. TEN PLAGUES ON EGYPT: Send tape recording to a missionary who is being persecuted.

22. QUAILS AND MANNA: Bring food for needy.

23. TABERNACLE BUILT: Make a model tabernacle.

24. TEN COMMANDMENTS: Write a note to your parents telling them you love and want to obey them in doing right.

25. NADAB AND ABIHU OFFER STRANGE FIRE: Write a letter to your elders telling them you want to always follow God's way.

26. SPIES IN CANAAN: Make a welcome card for a newcomer.

27. BALAAM BLESSES ISRAEL INSTEAD OF ENEMY: Write a puppet play about standing alone for what Jesus would want. Perform it for a younger class.

28. MOSES DIES AFTER 40 YEARS LEADING WANDERING JEWS: Make cards for elderly Christians thanking them for being faithful so long.

29. TWO SPIES SENT INTO CANAAN: Make thank you cards for someone keeping foster children.

30. JOSHUA MARCHES AROUND JERICHO: Make bumper or window stickers about loving and following God or about God's love and power.

31. ACHAN STEALS AND MAKES ISRAEL FALL IN BATTLE: Write a note to someone from whom you borrowed something saying you'll return it this week.

32. SUN AND MOON STAND STILL: Make some overhead transparencies showing how science and the Bible agree. Show them to your parents.

33. DEBORAH AND BARAK CONQUER CANAANITES: Make a poster about fighting sin.

34. GIDEON AND MIDIANITE MULTITUDE: Go somewhere where people walk by and hand them invitations to worship.

35. SAMSON'S STRENGTH: Plan a class party that will build up Christianity.

36. RUTH MARRIES A PRINCE: Make a card to send a newly

wed couple. Go to newspaper to find one if necessary.

37. SAMUEL BORN AND DEDICATED: Write this story as a play and put it on a tape recorder for a younger class.

38. SAUL ANOINTED KING: Write a letter to your mayor.

39. SAUL BECOMES ARROGANT AND DISOBEDIENT: Write a note to someone you disobeyed this week and say you'll do better.

40. DAVID SECRETLY ANOINTED KING: Write a letter to the President or Prime Minister.

41. DAVID KILLS GOLIATH: Send an invitation to worship to a grown up.

42. SAUL TRIES TO KILL DAVID: Send a note to someone being treated badly for doing good.

43. DAVID BECOMES KING: Write a letter to someone with a lot of money and thank them for remaining Christian.

44. DAVID AND BATHSHEBA: If you have something that is not belong to you, write a note to the owner saying you'll return it.

45. ABSALOM TRIES TO STEAL THE KINGDOM: Write a letter to your parents telling them you love them.

46. DAVID GIVES THRONE TO SOLOMON: Write someone you want to be like when you grow up.

47. SOLOMON CHOOSES WISDOM: Bring pictures of nature to send a missionary for their Bible class material.

48. THE TEMPLE IS BUILT: Make a model temple.

49. SOLOMON'S RICHES: Bring money to mail pictures to a missionary.

50. CIVIL WAR DIVIDES ISRAEL: Write a missionary in a war-torn land.

51. NORTHERN KINGDOM WORSHIPS CALF: Make a tape of your class singing and give it to a shut-in.

52. AHAB AND JEZEBEL STEAL A VINEYARD: Bring food for the needy.

53. ELIJAH DESTROYS BALL WORSHIPPERS: Record a devotional on tape and send or take it to a shut-in.

54. ELIJAH GOES TO HEAVEN IN CHARIOT OF FIRE: Write a sympathy/encouragement card to family of a deceased Christian.

55. ELISHA INCREASES WIDOW'S OIL: Bring some food for needy.

56. ELISHA RAISES SHUNAMITE SON: Make sympathy card to family whose child has gone to heaven. Tell about the resurrection.

57. NAAMAN'S LEPROSY HEALED: Make a get-well card for

someone.

58. INVISIBLE CHARIOTS CONQUER SAMARITANS AND SYRIANS: Send a letter to a serviceman away from home.

59. ASSYRIANS CAPTURE NORTHERN KINGDOM: Make as many invitations to church as possible to put on doors of houses near the church building.

60. ASA DESTROYS IDOLS IN SOUTHERN KINGDOM: Make posters about today's idols.

61. JOASH SAVED FROM WICKED GRANDMOTHER: Write a letter or card to your grandmother who is nice to you.

62. JOASH REFORMS JUDAH AT 20: Do some cleaning work in or around your church building.

63. UZZIAH LEAVES GOD AND GETS LEPROSY: Send get-well cards.

64. AHAZ WORSHIPS IDOLS: Write a missionary who works in a country that has idols.

65. HEZEKIAH REOPENS THE TEMPLE: Clean part of the church building.

66. HEZEKIAH'S LIFE EXTENDED 15 YEARS: Make hospital tray favors.

67. MANASSEH MARTYRS ISAIAH: Write thank you letter to elders who lead us to stand up for right.

68. UZZIAH REFORMS JUDAH: Send church tracts to the parents of your friends.

69. JEHOIAKIM TRIES TO KILL JEREMIAH: Write thank you letter to your minister.

70. EZRA REBUILDS TEMPLE: Do some work in the church building to fix it up.

71. NEHEMIAH REBUILDS JERUSALEM WALLS: Do some work on the church building yard.

72. QUEEN ESTHER SAVES THE JEWS: Write a letter of appreciation to the elders' wives.

73. JOB SUFFERS PATIENTLY: Send get-well card to someone.

74. DAVID WRITES PSALMS: Sing and teach songs to a younger class.

75. SOLOMON WRITES PROVERBS: Make a scrap book about proverbs to send assisted-care home residents.

76. ISAIAH PROPHECIES CHRIST: Bring pictures to send a missionary to help teach about God to children there.

77. JEREMIAH JAILED FOR WARNING KINGS: Write a letter to

the editor about our nation's need for God.

78. EZEKIEL SEES INTO HEAVEN: Write poems about heaven to send nursing home patients.

79. DANIEL AND FRIENDS REFUSE KING'S JUNK FOOD: Bring food for needy.

80. THREE MEN SAVED IN FURNACE: Write a missionary's children and encourage them.

81. WRITING ON THE WALL: Send invitations to Bible class to friends.

82. HOSEA DEPICTS UNFAITHFUL WIFE, ISRAEL: Make cards for newly weds.

83. JOEL PREDICTS HOLY SPIRIT: Make bookmarks for Bibles, the Sword of the Spirit.

84. AMOS WARNS ISRAEL OF DOOM: Write a letter to a friend who no longer comes to Bible class.

85. OBADIAH PREDICTS DOOM OF EDOMITES (ESAUITES): Write to a church in a mission area of the U.S. and ask what it is like.

86. JONAH SWALLOWED BY FISH: Cut out pictures to send a missionary for Bible class materials.

87. MICAH PREDICTS JESUS BORN AT BETHLEHEM: Make a birthday card to send someone special.

88. NAHUM PREDICTS FALL OF NINEVEH: Write a prison ministry and ask what it is like working with ex-convicts.

89. HABAKKUK PREDICTS INVASION OF SOUTHERN KINGDOM: Write a congregation in a war-torn country and encourage them.

90. ZEPHANIAH PREDICTS A FEW JEWS WILL RETURN: Call absentees on church office phone and tell them you miss them.

91. HAGGAI ENCOURAGES REBUILDING TEMPLE: Make something for your church building.

92. ZECHARIAH ENCOURAGES REBUILDING TEMPLE: Redecorate classroom.

93. MALACHI PREDICTS ELIJAH (JOHN) WILL INTRODUCE SAVIOR: Write and record a skit and ask a local radio station it if can be aired.

94. JESUS IS BORN: Make a toy or mobile for a baby.

95. JESUS TO TEMPLE AT 12: Write letter to your parents explaining how you love the church.

96. JESUS BAPTIZED: Examine the baptistery.

97. JESUS TEMPTED: Make a list of magazines you do not think

should be sold at a local store and send it to the owner.

98. FIRST MIRACLE IN CANA: Plan a snack and songs for younger class.

99. CLEANSES TEMPLE OF THIEVES: Bring money to buy Bibles for Eastern Europe or some other place where Bibles are hard to find for purchase.

100. TALKS WITH SAMARITAN WOMAN: Send letter to children worshipping in another land and try to become pen pals.

101. NOBLEMAN'S SON HEALED: Send favors to children's ward of hospital.

102. HEALS WITHERED HANDS ON SABBATH: Send cards to sick.

103. SENDS OUT APOSTLES BY TWOS: Write cards of appreciation to your deacons.

104. SERMON ON THE MOUNT: Make overhead transparencies describing different points in this sermon and ask the preacher if they could be used in one of his sermons

105. JOHN THE BAPTIST BEHEADED: Plan a class party with Christ-like things to do.

106. STORM CALMED: Make a scrap book of God's power over nature to give residents of an assisted-living home.

107. JAIRUS' DAUGHTER RAISED: Send favors or cards to children in the hospital.

108. 5000 FED: Bring food for needy.

109. TRANSFIGURATION: Bring money for Bibles to declare God's word for people in Eastern Europe or where ever Bibles are hard to find.

110. SPEAKS IN PARABLES: Write present-day parables and ask if they can be put in bulletin.

111. GOOD SAMARITAN: Make love cards for children of a church with another nationality.

112. PRODIGAL SON: Make and send cards to someone in a juvenile home.

113. RICH YOUNG RULER: Bring a toy you enjoy to give children in the hospital.

114. RICH MAN AND LAZARUS: Bring clothes or food for needy.

115. TEN LEPERS HEALED: Send tray favors to a hospital.

116. BLIND MAN HEALED: Bring money for Braille Bible or make a Braille I Love You card.

117. LAZARUS RAISED FROM DEAD: Make sympathy card and talk about our resurrection in it.

118. ZACCHAEUS: Make a banner about Jesus' love and hang it in church lobby one week.

119. TRIUMPHAL ENTRY INTO JERUSALEM: Have sidewalk parade for a couple blocks, carrying banners and singing or enter local town parade.

120. TEMPLE CLEANSED - WIDOW'S MITE: Bring money for Bibles to give away.

121. PARABLE OF THE VIRGINS: Send cards to newly weds.

122. PARABLE OF THE TALENTS: Look through Christian college yearbooks or other picture sources to see what it is like to be educated in that atmosphere.

123. LAST SUPPER: Examine elements of the Lord's Supper.

124. AGONY IN GETHSEMANE: Send a note to someone being treated badly for doing good.

125. JESUS' TRIAL: Write a local judge and thank him for being just and invite him to services.

126. JESUS CRUCIFIXION: Write poems about Jesus' death. Ask if they can be printed in the newspaper.

127. JESUS' RESURRECTION: Send sympathy cards and talk about heaven.

128. JESUS APPEARS TO DISCIPLES: Sing songs of Jesus on tape and send to a shut-in.

129. JESUS' ASSENSION TO HEAVEN: Pick a folk tune and make up words to it about Jesus going to heaven. Sing it to a class of adults.

130. THE CHURCH BEGINS ON PENTECOST: Mark map of world showing where different major languages are spoken.

131. PETER AND JOHN IMPRISONED: Write a missionary working near or in a nation hostile to Christians.

132. ANANIAS AND SAPPHIRE: Bring money you earned his week to buy Bibles to give away.

133. STEPHEN STONED: Write a missionary who works with Jews or Muslims.

134. ETHIOPIAN EUNUCH CONVERTED: Write a black preacher or congregation in Africa a thank-you note for their faithfulness.

135. SAUL CONVERTED: Write editor of a Christian magazine a thank-you note.

136. PETER RAISES DORCAS: Send letters of thank you to elderly Christian lady who helps others.

137. GENTILE CORNELIUS CONVERTED: Write a serviceman away from home.

138. JAMES KILLED, PETER IMPRISONED: Write someone in jail telling them Jesus loves them.

139. GOVERNOR OF CYPRUS CONVERTED: Write your governor/premier and say you are praying for him/her.

140. PAUL AND BARNABUS STONED AT LYSTRA: Write a missionary who was forced to leave a country for preaching.

141. THE MACEDONIAN CALL: Make invitations to worship to put up on grocery-store bulletin boards.

142. LYDIA CONVERTED: Bring material scraps for a quilt.

143. PHILIPPIAN JAILER CONVERTED: Write your Chief of Police and thank him for protecting you, and invite him to church services.

144. PAUL PREACHES IN ATHENS BEFORE IDOLS: Write an airport and bus station to see if you could place some tracts there.

145. DIANA IMAGES BURNED IN EPHESUS: Write a congregation in a country that has idols.

146. PAUL ARRESTED FOR PREACHING IN JERUSALEM: Pass out tracts at a place where people walk by.

147. PAUL BEFORE FELIX: Send a letter to a relative who is not a Christian explaining why Jesus loves them.

148. PAUL BEFORE FESTUS AND AGRIPPA: Write an advertisement for the newspaper asking people to come to worship.

149. SHIP WRECKED: Send cookies to a serviceman, possibly in the Navy.

150. PAUL WRITES LETTERS IN PRISON FROM ROME: Write a letter to someone in a juvenile home telling them God loves them.

151. ROMANS - SAVED BY GRACE: Write a new Christian telling them how happy you are for them.

152. 1 CORINTHIANS - BE MORAL AND LOVING: Write and act out a video taped skit about doing right when you friends try to get you to do wrong.

153. 2 CORINTHIANS - FORGIVENESS: Send a note to someone who offended you and say you forgive them and love them.

154. GALATIANS - FRUIT OF SPIRIT: Bring fruit, label them after the fruits of the Spirit, put them in a basket and give to a widow.

155. EPHESIANS - ARMOR OF GOD: Draw pictures of the armor

of God, and send them with a note to a Christian serviceman.
156. PHILIPPIANS - VIRTUES: Make posters depicting each of the Christian virtues to be put on a bulletin board.

157. COLOSSIANS - JESUS' DIVINITY: Write poems about believing in Jesus and ask if they can be printed in the church bulletin.

158. 1 THESSALONIANS - CHRISTIANS' RESURRECTION: Make pictures of our resurrection to send to residents of a nursing home.

159. 2 THESSALONIANS - FALSE TEACHERS: Write a newspaper ad telling people to read the Bible for themselves, and to come to church.

160. 1 TIMOTHY - FAITHFUL MOTHER: Write a note of encouragement to a lady raising her children alone

161. 2 TIMOTHY - FAITHFUL TO DEATH: Write an older Christian thanking them for remaining faithful all their lives.

162. TITUS - ELDERS AND DEACONS: Write the elders' and deacons' wives thanking them for assisting their husbands.

163. PHILEMON - RUNAWAY: Send notes about God's love to send to an organization working with teen runaways.

164. HEBREWS - LAW FULFILLED: Make transparencies comparing the Jewish and Christian (material and spiritual) blessings and ask the preacher if he'd like to use them in a sermon.

165. JAMES - FAITH AND WORKS: Take photos of your class doing good works to send to local newspaper.

166. 1 PETER - PERSECUTION: Send notes about God's love to a juvenile home.

167. 2 PETER - FALSE TEACHERS: Sing a song about following the Bible and ask a local radio station if it can be aired.

168. 1 JOHN - JESUS' IS GOD: Write thank-you notes to Jesus for coming to earth to show us how to live and ask If they can be printed in the bulletin.

169. 2 JOHN - CHRISTIAN WOMAN: Send thank-you notes to Christian lady you know who does a lot of Christian works.

170. 3 JOHN - FELLOW WORKERS: Write notes to your elders thanking them for leading the congregation to help missionaries.

171. JUDE - STAND UP FOR JESUS: Record songs about standing up for Jesus and send to a shut-in.

172. TIMOTHY: Write encouragement notes to a woman raising her children alone.

173. TITUS: Write a thank-you note to your youth director or someone who helps the young people.

174. PHILEMON AND HIS RUNAWAY SLAVE: Contact an organization that works with runaways, and send them notes for them saying God loves them.

175. JOHN ON THE ISLE OF PATMOS: Write poems about heaven and send them to residents of a nursing home.

Appendix B
THEY WORSHIP IN A
NURSING HOME

Some shuffle, some lean on walkers, some are pushed in wheelchairs. Arthritis-laden legs bend, backs strain, and with the aid of shaking hands they sink down now into their chairs. Racing heartbeats ease to a slower pace.

After a little rest, some are given songbooks. The others cannot see. The first song is announced. Quivering lips part, cracking voices begin, and heaven opens. A chorus fit for the King of Glory rises through the ceiling of the little room, bursts into the universe, and swirls into the Divine throne room. The voices of gallant warriors, torn and broken in body. The voices of strong warriors, courageous to the very finish. The halting voices of conquerors boldly reaching for the crown.

A little later they hear the words, "We are gathered around this table to once again commemorate our Lord's death." Once again. Yes, once again as many times as it takes until the victory is reached.

Bent hands, stabbed still by throbbing arthritis and shaking with palsy, reach out to touch the first symbol. The bread has already been broken for them. Yet it is with determination that each forces fingers to close around the little fragment representing that crucified Body. Slowly, slowly it is taken up to the lips. Some fingers fumble at this point, and the fragment drops into a lap. The painful procedure is again repeated until completed.

Next the cup is brought. Blood symbol. Symbol of death and life. The little glass is so small it could embarrassingly spill. A kind friend picks it up and places it into the palm of the awaiting cupped hand. It is still shaking. So two hands are used ~ one folded under the first to steady it. The drink successfully reaches the lips and its contents triumphantly sipped. Oh what glory to still be able to honor the dying Savior after all these years! The glass falls out of tottering hands. It is caught by the tray. But the mind has already started transcending this room for another far above.

"Each week we give our contribution to a worthy cause," they hear explained. Presently the collection tray is brought around. Dimes and quarters are brought out of coin purses, shallow pockets, envelopes, Bible leaves. Some are wadded in cold hands. A faithful wife slips a dollar bill into the hand of her nearly paralyzed husband. Ever so slowly coins and dollar bills are carefully placed into the tray. Not much? It will help a burned-out family in town.

The preacher now stands before the little assembly. Many shift. Seats are harder, circulation cramped, arthritis continues to distress aged joints. He reads about being taken home to Glory someday. Some watch him, some gaze at the floor. He speaks of heaven. They begin to feel left behind. They think of those they ache to see again. It has been so long. They've fought so many battles. A few tears slip down as due drops. They dream of heaven in the morning....

The sermon over, the last prayer said, they begin to leave. Slowly.... But it hadn't always been that way. In years past they had taken time out of busy weeks, gathered up their freshly scrubbed children, and gone down the road to the church house. They had sung heartily and kept their children still. And afterward they had bustled about from one group to the other discussing crops or jobs, new recipes or styles, revivals or new buildings.

That was an eternity away. Now they await another eternity ~ it is much nearer. Dreams have been formed and some dissolved. Children born and some died. Homes built and some broken. Bodies that once were strong and vigorous, minds that once were full of exciting daily activities, spirits that once were robust. Now all are tired. No, they never reached perfection. Some still are impatient. Some still can't always tell the truth. Some still pout. Some occasionally lose tempers. All continue with faults. But because of it all, they are most grateful for Jesus' grace. Despite failings, He sees them as victors through Him, and loves them now as at the beginning.

The room is nearly empty now. They make their way down wandering halls to little rooms and resume their wait for the Mansions. They sigh. Battles of life have been met and fought. Mountains climbed. Desolations conquered. So now it is a matter of waiting and encouraging those left behind to do the best that they, too, can do. Tired. Waiting. But willing to go on until they touch the mark. And then….

And then…. they will start all over. Only this time it will be different. For this time there will be no pain, no foes, no failures, and never again will they grow old!

~Katheryn Maddox Haddad

Appendix C
LOST LOVED ONES:
HARD QUESTIONS ANSWERED

Please do not consider this something that is just nice to read. It is here to expand your understanding of the chapter on "Loss of Loved Ones." It is placed in the back as a handy reference for you in the future. Read it now, and keep it in mind for later use. There are always people with such questions. Here are some ways to answer those questions.

IF GOD IS SO GOOD, WHY DOES HE MAKE PEOPLE SUFFER AND DIE? God does not do this. Satan does this. Luke 13:16 tells of Satan causing a woman to suffer for 18 years, and there are numerous other examples of Satan causing suffering. In fact, Jesus healed people as an act of overcoming Satan's evil work. John 8:44 calls Satan a murderer.

To a Christian, death is not the enemy Satan intended it to be, for Jesus through his resurrection overcame death. *When the perishable has been clothed with the imperishable, and the mortal with immortality, then the saying that is written will come true: "Death has been swallowed up in victory. Where, O death, is your victory? Where, O death, is your sting? ....Thanks be to God! He gives us the victory through our Lord Jesus Christ" (Romans 8:28).*

What Satan meant for bad has been turned into good. Death is the only door into heaven. It takes courage to go to heaven, to go through that door, but it can be done, and it is worth it. Yes, the family left behind is painfully lonely, but is glad for the person who is now in heaven.

I JUST CAN'T BELIEVE THERE IS A GOD, BECAUSE IF HE EXISTED, MY CHILD WITH SO MANY YEARS AHEAD WOULD NOT HAVE DIED. I WILL NEVER SET FOOT IN A CHURCH BUILDING AGAIN. (This statement is usually made by people who do not attend church much to start with, and whose faith is very weak. Sometimes when people are not very close to God, God can use events that Satan means for bad to help people draw closer to him.)

Have you thought about God very much in the past few years ~ honestly? You're thinking about him now. You may be angry with God, but you are at least thinking about him. Sometimes it takes something startling like this to get our attention back on God. Now use that anger. Search to see if God really does love you and your child. The Bible will show you that he does.

A scripture from the book of Esther asks, *Who knows but that you have come...for such a time as this?* (4:14b). Now think of your child. Who knows but that your child was sent to you for such a time as this. With your faith weak, your child may be able to tell you now in a strong enough way, "God loves me and loves you too. I am with God now; so please love him back so you can be with us someday too." This may have been your child's entire purpose for having been given to you. Isn't that a wonderful purpose?

Compared with the incomprehensible millions of "years" in eternity, what are a few years on a temporary earth anyway? That child may have been saved from a lot of pain and heartache later on in this life. It is our eternal home that is important and best, and your child got to go there earlier than most. God does exist. And he has not cursed you, but blessed you.

MY DAD NEVER WENT TO CHURCH. DO YOU THINK HE HAS A CHANCE OF GOING TO HEAVEN? First, tell your friend you are not the judge; that God keeps all of that out of the hands of we humans with our frail minds. Then go on to explain that you understand there are levels of reward and punishment (refer to the parables of the talents and cities).

2 Peter 2:20f says, *If they have escaped the corruption of the world by knowing our Lord and Savior Jesus Christ and are again entangled in it and overcome, they are worse off at the end than they were at the beginning. It would have been better*
for them not to have known the way of righteousness than to have known it and then turn their backs on the sacred commandment that was passed on to them.

Also you may refer to Luke 16 but preface your statement with a reassurance that you are not saying where their father is. However, it does give us an example. The rich man went to hell, and there he remembered his family and begged Abraham to send someone back to warn them, for he still loved them and did not want the same thing to happen to them. This shows us that wherever our loved ones go, we can ease their minds somehow (somehow they are still aware of us, but to what extent we do not know) by following God's ways as closely as possible.

Finally, you can say that one thing we know for sure; we have a loving heavenly Father who is not wanting anyone to perish (2 Peter 3:9).

MY BABY WASN'T BAPTIZED. WILL THAT MAKE A DIFFERENCE? Ezekiel 18:2-4 says that the children will not bear the inherited sins of the fathers. The soul who sins is the one who will die. In Mark 10:15, Jesus said in order to enter the kingdom of God we must be like a little child. Peter said in Acts 2:38, *Repent, and be baptized, every one of you, in the name of Jesus Christ so that your sins may be forgiven.* A child has no sins and therefore cannot repent of them, neither is it old enough to understand what baptism is all about anyway. Your baby is safe in the arms of Jesus.

WHAT IS DYING LIKE? The example of the rich man and Lazarus noted above tells us. When Lazarus died angels carried him to Abraham's side (Luke 16:22). Hebrews 1:14 asks rhetorically, *Are not all angels ministering spirits sent to serve those who will inherit salvation?* It makes sense, then, that if we have angels (and perhaps each of us with a particular angel) watching over us, that is the angel who comes and gets us for the "crossing over."

Is it dark? Many people refer to having courage when passing through the valley of the shadow of death (Psalm 23). However, Amos 5:8 says the Lord turns the shadow of death into the morning, and Matthew 4:16 announced, *To them which sat in the region and shadow of death light is sprung up* (KJV). Of course we remember Revelation 21:23: The city does not need the sun or the moon to shine on it, for the glory of God gives it light, and the Lamb is its lamp.

WHERE DOES A PERSON GO WHEN THEY FIRST DIE? Jesus told the thief on the cross (who was still living in the Jewish era, not the Christian era of baptism) that when they died he would be with him in paradise. Paul said that he was caught up to paradise, which he also called the third heaven (2 Corinthians 12:1-4) but saw things he was not allowed to tell.

Revelation 2:7 says the tree of life is in the paradise of God, and 22:14 says those who gain the right to the tree of life may go on into the city of God. It seems that paradise is for the saved awaiting the Day of Judgment when final sentence/reward is to be pronounced and given. Also, according to the rich man and Lazarus, there seems to be an awareness of those awaiting hell in *gehenna*, and also of people left behind on earth.

However, Revelation 22:2 says the tree of life is growing on either side of the river of life which flows forth from the throne of God which is, of course, in heaven. Further, Revelation 10:6 says there will be time no more. So, perhaps the Day of Judgment occurs as soon as someone dies and is no longer in the realm of time, and paradise is now part of heaven.

WILL WE KNOW EACH OTHER IN HEAVEN? Jesus said that people from all over the earth would take their place in the kingdom of heaven along with Abraham, Isaac and Jacob (Matthew 8:11). Jesus, while on earth, had an extensive conversation with Moses and Elijah long after the two prophets had died; they had kept their identity. (See Matthew 17:3.) And, back to Jesus' reference to the rich man and Lazarus, they still were identified as the same people. All of these kept their identity.

IF MY SISTER DIES AND GOES TO HELL AND I DIE AND GO TO HEAVEN, HOW CAN I BE HAPPY KNOWING WHERE SHE IS? Revelation 21:4 promises, *He will wipe every tear from their eyes. There will be no more death or mourning or crying or pain, for the old order of things has passed away.* If there is no mourning, this would mean that God will have a way of eliminating the memory of people who are not there in heaven.

WHAT IS HEAVEN LIKE? Descriptions of heaven are found in Revelation 4, 21 and 22. Although these have a symbolic meaning, there is probably a literal meaning of some kind that could relate to a spirit(ual) world. There are twelve kinds of precious foundation stones. The gates are of pearl, the wall of diamond, the streets and city of gold. God's throne is diamond, encircled with seven great spirit lights, over that is a ruby glow, and over all of it an emerald rainbow.

WHAT WILL WE LOOK LIKE IN HEAVEN? John 14:2 says so beautifully that there are many mansions prepared for God's children in heaven. We usually think of them as houses for our spiritual bodies to dwell in; however, these are houses for our spirits to dwell in, just like our present bodies of clay are just houses for our eternal spirits. Aging Peter referred in 2 Peter 1:14 and 15 to putting off the present tabernacle [tent] of his body and dying.

Paul explained in 2 Corinthians 5:1-4: *Now we know that if the earthly tent [temporary] we live in is destroyed, we have a building [permanent] from God, an eternal house in heaven, not built by human hands. Meanwhile, we groan, longing to be clothed with our heavenly dwelling, because when we are clothed, we will not be found naked. For while we are in this tent, we groan and are burdened, because we do not wish to be unclothed but to be clothed with our heavenly dwelling, so that what is mortal may be swallowed up by life.*

1 Corinthians 15:35-38, 42-44,49 further explains: *But someone may ask, "How are the dead raised? With what kind of body will they come?" How foolish! What you sow does not come to life unless it dies. When you sow, you do not plant the body that will be, but just a seed, perhaps of wheat or of something else. But God gives it a body as he has determined, and to each kind of seed he gives its own body. So will it be with the resurrection of the dead. The body that is sown perishable, it is raised imperishable; it is sown in dishonor, it is raised in glory; it is sown in weakness, it is raised in power; it is sown a natural body, it is raised a spiritual body. And just as we have borne the likeness of the earthly man, so shall we bear the likeness of the man from heaven.*

. *"But our citizenship is in heaven. We eagerly await a Savior from there, the Lord Jesus Christ, who, by the power that enables him to bring everything under his control, will transform our lowly bodies so that they will be like his glorious body"* (Philippians 3:20-21).

What was Jesus' glorious body like? His body could walk on water (Matthew 14:24f), it could glow like the sun (Mark 9:2-8), it could become invisible (Luke 4:28-30), it could walk through walls (John 20:19), it could not decay (Acts 2:3), it could change shape (John 20:14-16; John 21:3-7; Luke 24:15-16, his body could soar (Acts 1:9) it will be recognized by everyone (Revelation 1:7).

Thank You

Thanks for reading my book! I'm so honored that you chose to spend your precious time with my research and experiences. You are appreciated. I'm an independent author who relies on my readers to help spread the word about stories you enjoy. Would you take a few minutes to let your friends know on Facebook, Pinterest... wherever you hang out online?

Also, each honest review at online retailers means a lot to me and helps other readers know if this is a book they might enjoy,

I welcome contact from readers. At my website (below), you can do so. You can also sign up for my newsletter (below) to be notified of half-price books and new releases.

About the Author

Katheryn Maddox Haddad grew up in the cold north and now lives in Arizona where she does not have to shovel sunshine. She basks in 100-degree weather with palm trees, cacti, and a computer with most of the lettering worn off.

She has a bachelor's degree in English, Bible, and social science, from Harding University, a Master's Degree in management and human relations from Abilene Christian University, and part of a Master's Degree in Bible from Harding University, including Greek studies.

She spends half her day writing, and the other half teaching English over the internet worldwide using the Bible as textbook through World English Institute. She has taught some 7000 Muslims, mostly in the Middle East. Students she has converted to Christianity are in hiding in Afghanistan, Iran, Iraq, Yemen, Jordan, Somalia, Sierra Leone, Uzbekistan, Tajikistan, Indonesia, and Palestine. "They are my heroes," she says.

In addition to her seventy-seven books (non-fiction, novels, and storybooks), she has written numerous articles for *Gospel Advocate, Twentieth Century Christian, Firm Foundation, Christian Bible Teacher, Christian Woman,* and several world mission publications. Her weekly column, *Little-Known Facts About the Bible,* appeared several years in newspapers in North Carolina and Texas.

BUY YOUR NEXT BOOK NOW

CHRISTIAN LIFE
Applied Christianity: Handbook 500 Good Works
You Can Be a Hero Alone
Worship Changes Since 1st Century + Worship 1sr Century Way
The Best of Alexander Campbell's Millennial Harbinger
Inside the Hearts of Bible Women-Reader+Audio+Leader
The Lord's Supper: 52 Readings with Prayers
http://bit.ly/Christianlife

BIBLE TEXT STUDIES
Revelation: A Love Letter From God
The Holy Spirit: 592 Verses Examined
Was Jesus God? (Why Evil)
365 Life-Changing Scriptures Day by Date
Love Letters of Jesus & His Bride, Ecclesia
Christianity or Islam? The Contrast
The Road to Heaven
http://bit.ly/BibleTexts

FUN BOOKS
Bible Puzzles, Bible Song Book, Bible Numbers
http://bit.ly/BibleFun

TOUCHING GOD SERIES
365 Golden Bible Thoughts: God's Heart to Yours
365 Pearls of Wisdom: God's Soul to Yours
365 Silver-Winged Prayers: Your Spirit to God's
http://bit.ly/TouchingGodSeries

-SURVEY SERIES: EASY BIBLE WORKBOOKS
→Old Testament & New Testament Surveys
→Questions You Have Asked-Part I & II
http://bit.ly/BibleWorkbooks

HISTORICAL RESEARCH BIBLE
for Novel, Screenwriter, Documentary & Thesis Writers
http://bit.ly/32uZkHa

GENEALOGY: How to Climb Your Family Tree Without Falling Out
Volume I & 2: Beginner-Intermediate & Colonial-Medieval
http://bit.ly/GenealogyBeginner-Advanced

Connect With The Author

Website: **https://inspirationsbykatheryn.com**

Facebook: **bit.ly/FacebooksKatherynMaddoxHaddad**

Linkedin: **http://bit.ly/KatherynLinkedin**

Twitter: **https://twitter.com/KatherynHaddad**

Pinterest: **https://www.pinterest.com/haddad1940/**

Goodreads:
https://www.goodreads.com/katherynmaddoxhaddad

Get A Free Book
Sign up for Katheryn's monthly newsletter with half-price books for the whole family and insider tips on what's coming next.
http://bit.ly/katheryn

Join My Dream Team
Members get the first peek at my newest book and have fun offering me advice sometimes. I have a point system of rewards for helping me get the word out. Check it out here: **http://bit.ly/KatherynsDreamTeam**